Country, Kin and Culture

Claire Smith is Professor in Archaeology at Flinders University, Adelaide, Australia. Accompanied by her husband, Gary Jackson, and son, Jimmy Smith, she has worked closely with the Barunga, Manyallaluk and Wugularr communities every year since 1990.

This book is dedicated to four old ladies: Lily Willika, whom I called grandmother; Daisy Borduk, who decided to make sure that I had the true story; Glen Wesan, who calls me 'talk-talk'; and Phyllis Wiynjorroc, who named my son after her father, Lamjerroc.

This book also is dedicated to Muriel Taylor and Annette Smith.

Country, Kin and Culture

Survival of an Australian Aboriginal Community

Claire Smith

Wakefield Press

Wakefield Press
16 Rose Street
Mile End
South Australia 5031
www.wakefieldpress.com.au

First published 2004
Reprinted 2020

Designed by Clinton Ellicott, Wakefield Press

National Library of Australia
Cataloguing-in-publication entry

Smith, Claire, 1957– .
Country, kin and culture: survival of an Australian Aboriginal community.

ISBN 978 1 86254 575 5.

1. Aboriginal Australians – Northern Territory – Barunga Region – History. 2. Aboriginal Australians – Northern Territory – Barunga Region – Social life and customs. I. Title.

306.089991594295

Wakefield Press thanks
Coriole Vineyards for
continued support

Contents

Preface

This book arises from my research with the Barunga–Wugularr community of the Northern Territory, Australia. My husband Gary Jackson, son, Jimmy, and I lived there for more than a year during 1991 and 1992. Since then we have returned every year, sometimes for periods of several months. And most years, Aboriginal people from the region have come to stay with us. Slowly, inexorably, we became a small part of an extended community. During this time we learnt that community is not a place but a network of people. The way in which Barunga and Wugularr people live the notion of community is much more fluid than the way in which Europeans conceive of this. Community is part of a cultural landscape that dissolves geographic boundaries. This landscape includes not only geographic areas and landmarks but kinship networks. The Barunga–Wugularr community is not located only at Barunga or Wugularr. It is located at the neighbouring settlements of Manyallaluk and Gulin Gulin; at the outstations of Weemol and Gropulyu and Blue Water; at Katherine and the satellite Aboriginal settlements of 'Rockhole' and 'Gorge Camp'; at Darwin; at Adelaide; and where-ever people live who have kinship ties to Barunga. The common link is family. Aboriginal people are born into extended kinship networks and with relatives who live in a number of places, remote, rural and urban. From this point of view, the Barunga–Wugularr community also resides with members of the stolen generation, some of whom may be unaware of their

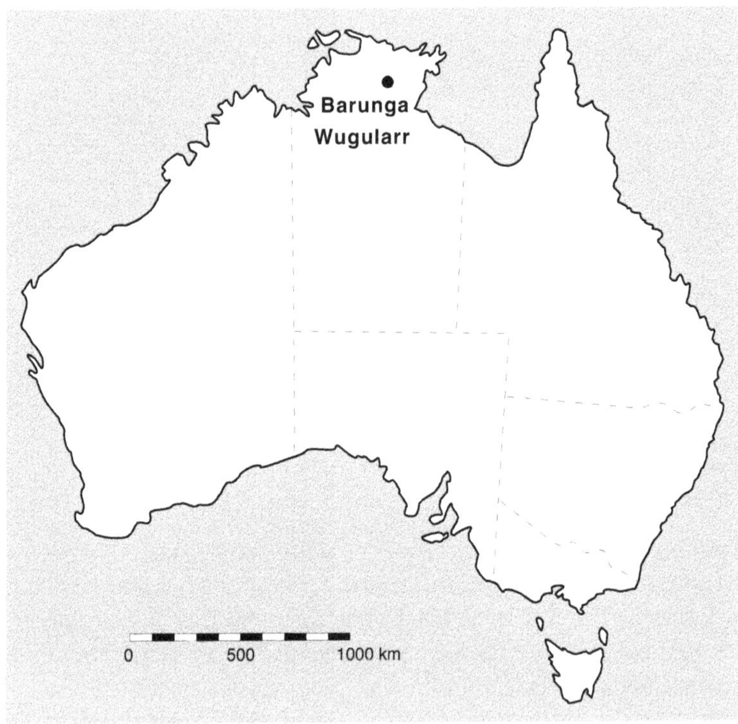

Location of Barunga and Wugularr

ties but who nevertheless are an important part of the cultural landscape of their kin.

It wasn't my idea to write this book. I am an archaeologist, not an historian. However, Aboriginal people rarely draw the sharp disciplinary boundaries that are so essential to a European way of thinking and my lack of formal training as an historian did not dissuade my mentors at Barunga and Wugularr from telling me that I should write this history book. In particular, this book was instigated by Daisy Borduk, a very special old lady who took on the onerous task of making sure that my husband and I recorded the history of country, kin and culture. I was also encouraged to write this book by Phyllis Wiyjorroc, the senior traditional owner for the Barunga–Wugularr region, and senior custodians, Peter Manabaru, Paddy Babu, Lily Willika, Lily Bennett and Victor Hood as well as Jimmy Wesan and his wife Glen. I am grateful to the entire Willika family for being such good friends.

Beswick Falls
Photo: Donna Flood

The scope of this book broadened considerably during 1998, after I got to know Eileen Cummings, Irene Fisher and Lorraine Siwers. Around this time I also met Rita Tingey, who was removed from her mother, Daisy Borduk, when she was a child. My conversations with Eileen and Lorky, in particular, made me aware of how government policies had controlled so many fundamental aspects of Aboriginal people's lives. My decision to re-write the book in order to address these human rights issues was reinforced with a challenge by Aileen Morton-Robinson to deal with the idea of 'whiteness'. This produced a more critical work as well as the chapter on stolen generations.

The other impetus to write this book came from my being awarded the inaugural David Phillipps prize for a postgraduate thesis in Aboriginal studies at the University of New England. This award was established by David's wife, Anna. David Phillipps was a renaissance scholar, fluent in French and German, as well as Latin and Greek. He is described by his friend David Farrell as 'a writer, poet, historian, critic and playwright', a man who devoted his time to teaching postgraduate students with 'care, devotion and immense satisfaction'. He was also a man with a strong sense of social justice, as demonstrated by his wife's decision to honour his memory through supporting the publication of a research series in Aboriginal studies, with the aim of sharing academic knowledge in this area with the wider community. This book is one part of David Phillipps' legacy.

The research for this book was undertaken over 12 years. It was funded by the Australian Research Council, the Australian Institute of Aboriginal Studies, Flinders University, the University of New England, the Australian Institute of Nuclear Science and Engineering and the Ian Potter Foundation.

Finally, I would like to thank Heather Burke and Antoinette Hennessey, who drew the figures for this book. My husband, anthropologist Gary Jackson, has conducted the research with me every year since 1990.

Claire Smith
College of Humanities, Arts and Social Sciences
Flinders University
South Australia
Claire.Smith@flinders.edu.au

This book has been written under the guidance of Phyllis Wiynjorroc, Peter Manabaru and Jimmy Wesan.

One

Contact and Conflict

Sickly sentiment and Exeter Hall humanitarianism should be valued at their true worth, our European settlers must be allowed to till the soil and extract the wealth from the land which they have made their home, free from the murdering raids of these savages.

(Editorial, *Northern Territory Times and Gazette*, 4th October 1884)

Before Invasion

Indigenous Australians have occupied the mainland and islands of Australia for at least the past 50,000 years. During this time they have developed subtle and complex social systems and their own unique solutions to the range of climates and environments offered by the Australian continent. The achievements of these first Australians include what were probably the earliest planned sea voyages by people anywhere in the world; the earliest examples of deliberate human burials as part of spiritual/religious ceremonies; some of the earliest rock art and items of personal adornment; and the first boomerangs, ground-edge axes and grindstones.[1] In keeping with these remarkable achievements, Aboriginal cultures were highly dynamic and adaptable. For thousands of years Aboriginal groups had been influencing each other and had maintained considerable contact with Melanesian and Indonesian traders long before the first British colonists landed at Sydney Cove. Change was characteristic of Aboriginal social systems, as was a flexibility which allowed core social structures to endure by being fine tuned to suit new circumstances. This intellectual and physical adaptability enabled Indigenous Australians to find the resilience and strength to survive the period of contact with the British colonisers.

A common misconception held by the British at contact, and long afterwards, is that Indigenous Australians were a unified, relatively homogeneous group of people. Throughout the world European worldviews consistently incorporated the diversity of individual Indigenous populations into a single category, such as 'Indian', or 'Aboriginal'. This arose from, and reinforced, the colonial notion of Indigenous peoples as 'other', as something different to 'self', which was assumed to be European – a notion used to justify different treatment of Indigenous and *non*-Indigenous peoples. The collapse of independent Indigenous societies into a homogeneous whole worked for government bodies, as it facilitated the easy administration of Indigenous peoples. It is a powerful symbol of the loss of identity that Indigenous peoples endured as a result of invasion. This notion of Indigenous homogeneity has been criticised by many scholars on the grounds that it masks not only the diversity of Indigenous cultures but also the political autonomy and processes of self-government that were in place in Indigenous societies prior to European invasion.

In fact, at contact there were extensive differences in the social organisation and cultural practices of Aboriginal peoples across Australia, differences continually reinforced and negotiated through language, art and ritual. The Indigenous societies encountered by the British contained some of the most complex and refined social structures in the world. However, Europeans judged to be sophisticated only those societies which valued and produced an elaborate material culture, such as palaces and pyramids, and because Indigenous societies had produced no monuments of this kind, Europeans assumed that these people were 'backward' or 'primitive'. In fact, the opposite was the case: the human intellect and energy that Europeans had put into building sophisticated and elegant material edifices were used by Indigenous Australians to build sophisticated and elegant social and intellectual edifices. The irony here is that Europeans were judging cultural complexity purely on the basis of material goods – and that the cultural, social and intellectual complexity of Indigenous Australian groups far exceeded that of European cultures, either then or now.

A Subtle and Sophisticated Social System[2]

Indigenous Australians have always led sophisticated and culturally rich lives. The structure of Indigenous societies at contact was founded on the relationships between people, their kin and the land, determining every person's relationship to the world around them – to other people; to plants and animals; and to the past, present and future. All of these relationships involve very specific rights, obligations and rules of behaviour and are an inherent part of the lives of people living in the Barunga–Wugularr region today.

During the creation era known by Europeans as the Dreaming or Dreamtime,[3] ancestral beings travelled the land, creating its topographic features until at last 'sitting down' to become forever part of a specific place. Tracks established by ancestral beings during the Dreaming are woven through this landscape and formed the religious basis for extended communication networks. Some of these Dreaming tracks span the entire Australian continent, one stretching from the 'Top End' of the Northern Territory to the South Australian coast. Other tracks were more locally based, connecting Dreaming sites within a particular region. The Dreaming is both 'then' and 'now'. It encompasses events of the ancestral past but also exists in the present.

Figure 1.1
Rock painting of 'Luma Luma', an ancestral figure that travelled through the Barunga–Wugularr region in the Dreaming era

Figure 1.2
Dreaming site of female ancestral being on the road between Barunga and Wugularr

Within the Indigenous Australian cosmos, power flows from inherently powerful ancestral beings to the land, which is imbued with a potency given to it by the actions of people and ancestors in the past. In this way, every facet of the landscape becomes imbued with ancestral associations and ascribed with social identity. This power then flows through to living people, some of whom have the ability to call upon the force and authority inherent in both the land and ancestral beings.

The land is an important part of Indigenous people's identities, closely tied to sophisticated social systems that structured relationships to country. In traditional society, an integral part of growing up is for people to learn about their relationships to country. As they move through their lands they learn about the relationships between place and ancestors, in the process learning about themselves and their particular rights and responsibilities to land. Rock-art sites play an important role in this process of identification. Kinship relationships link ancestors, contemporary peoples, specific places and wider 'country'. In this sense, there is no separation of land, kinship, inheritance or religion.

In contrast to Western systems of knowledge, which are grounded in the written word, Aboriginal knowledge systems are based primarily on oral traditions, and were communicated through dance, story, art and song. Such knowledge – of the past, of the land and its resources and of other groups of people – was, in fact, the major device used by Indigenous Australians to occupy the continent and successfully manage the range of environments. Oral traditions are far more fluid and subtle than written systems of communication. Oral forms of communication place power directly in the hands of senior people, who are the respected holders and interpreters of Indigenous law. In the Barunga–Wugularr region, religious and cultural knowledge is separated into 'women's business' and 'men's business'. Under this system the right to knowledge has to be achieved and information is revealed to people gradually, at particular stages in their life and as they prove themselves worthy of being entrusted with this information and its attendant responsibilities.

The kinship systems of Australia's Arnhem Land region are recognised by anthropologists as being among the most sophisticated and complex recorded anywhere in the world. The relationships between groups of people and between people and the land are structured along many planes. One of the most important of these is the language group, which affiliates people to traditional tracts of land or 'country'. People acquire language affiliation through having parents of a particular language group, who themselves are affiliated to the territory associated with that language group. Since 'Jawoyn-ness' or 'Ngalkpon-ness' can only be acquired as a birthright, people affiliated with a particular language group are necessarily the direct descendants of forebears who also belonged to that language group. Sometimes people may be given a choice of language group affiliation if their parents come from different language groups, although their choice of residence can also influence people in this matter. A person's language group is imposed to a large degree by family members, and is securely recognised by adolescence.

The traditional language group boundaries of the Barunga–Wugularr region are shown in Map 1.1, which is derived from the relevant sections of Tindale's[4] Australian Aboriginal language group map and adjusted according to a recent reassessment in Horton[5] and contemporary explanations by Aboriginal people of linguistic boundaries in the region.

Language group is closely related to clan membership, since a person's clan is also based upon his or her affiliation to particular

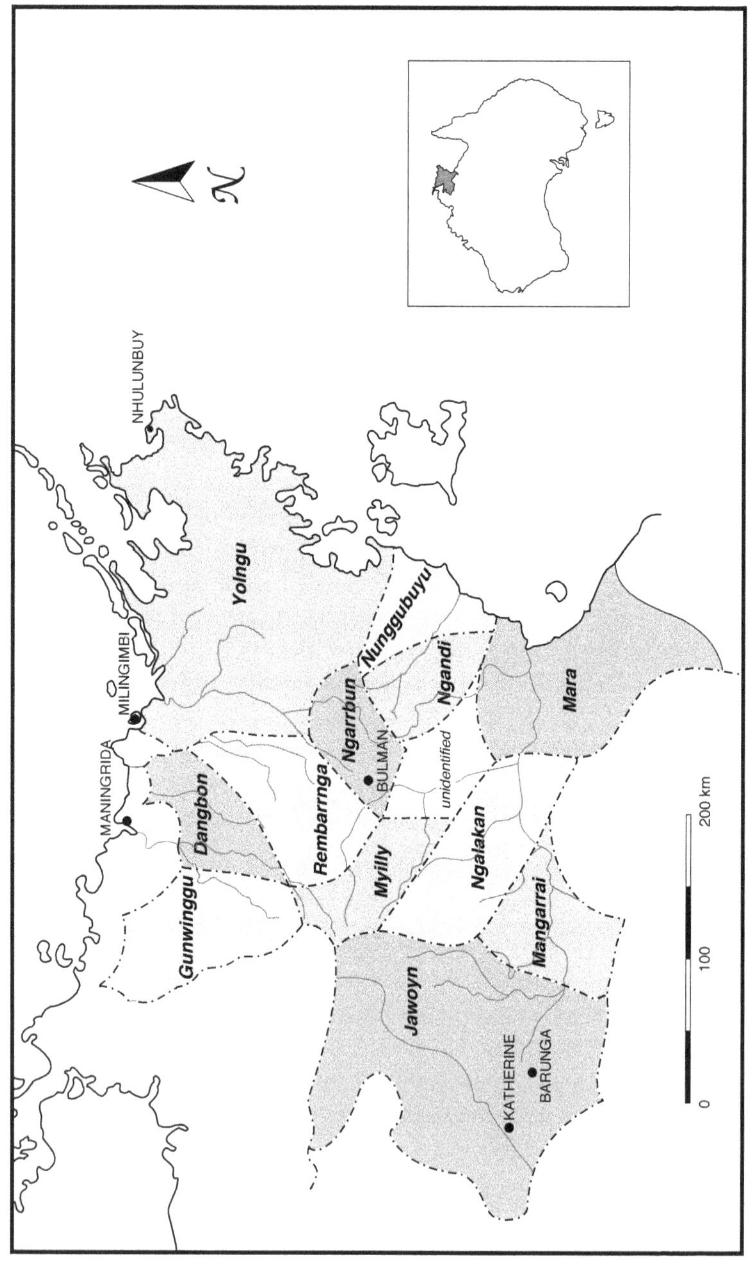

Map 1.1
Language group boundaries in the region

tracts of country. Thus, people of a particular clan will all belong to the same language group. Clan is inherited from the father, as are many clan designs used to depict country. Land is the common ground between the human members of the clan and the powers that gave the land its form, and it is these relationships which are played out in ceremonies.

A fundamental social division is that of moiety, which is an important means by which Barunga people perceive the world around them. During the Dreaming, ancestral beings assigned everything in the world – people, animals, plants, places – to either the Dhuwa or Yirritja moiety, each moiety being associated with particular colours and proportions. Dhuwa colours are those at the dark end of the spectrum, especially red and black, while Yirritja colours are those at the light end, especially yellow and white. Similarly, Dhuwa is associated with shortness and Yirritja with tallness. Thus, the black cockatoo is Dhuwa while the white cockatoo is Yirritja. Likewise, the short-necked turtle is Dhuwa and the long-necked turtle Yirritja.

One of the most important principles of society in the Barunga–Wugularr region is that of joining Dhuwa and Yirritja moieties so that they are 'in company'. This encompasses the idea of balance within the natural and cultural world. One of the clearest ways in which this is expressed is through the marriage system.

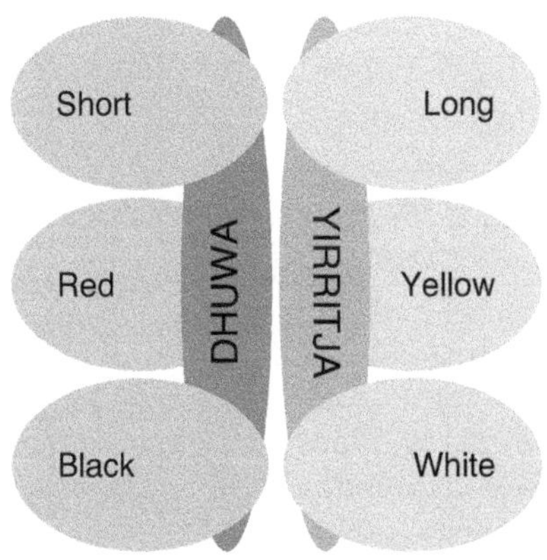

Figure 1.3
Relationships between moieties, colours and dimensions
Courtesy Global Books

People, like land, animals and plants, are born with moiety. The basic rules here are that a child's moiety will be the opposite of her mother, and thus the same as the father, and that a Dhuwa person should marry a Yirritja person. In this way, the relationships between child and mother and between husband and wife are founded on a harmonious symmetry that mirrors the equilibrium found in the natural world.

The rules for marriage, however, are more complex than this. The Ngalkpon social system, for example, is broken into 16 social divisions, called subsections by anthropologists and 'skin' by Aboriginal people, since this is what people are born with and cannot be changed. Skin is inherited from the mother. For Ngalkpon people, the skin system is arranged in two circles, each of which has eight groups. For example, a mother whose skin is Gotjan will have children whose skin is Beliny (female) or Balang (male). The children of the daughter whose skin is Beliny will be Bangirn (female) or Bangardi (male). The cycle continues until after several generations, Galijan, the daughter of Bangirn, is seen to be the mother of Gotjan. A separate system exists which provides comparable inherited links between mothers and children for the other eight skin groups.

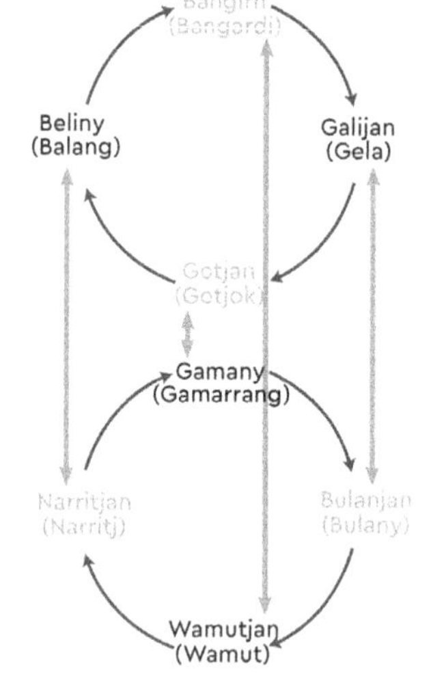

Figure 1.4
Subsection (skin) groups for Ngalkpon people

These two circles of skin relationships are joined in two principle ways; through marriage and through a reciprocal relationship between 'owners' and 'custodians' of cultural knowledge. In marriages, there are only two skin group categories from which an individual's partner can be selected. Both of these choices have to be made from the opposite skin group circle, minimising the possibility of incest within the mother's line. A consequence of this system was that men or women from the other six skin groups for each gender – that is, three-quarters of the population of the opposite sex – are prohibited as marriage partners. These very strict marriage rules serve to regulate social interactions, cementing kinship relationships and acting as a taboo against marriage between biologically close relations, even in those areas where population numbers are low.

Until very recently the penalties for marrying someone from another skin group were very harsh, and included death. Most people today still marry according to the correct skin group, but if children are born from a 'wrong' marriage involving two Yirritja or two Dhuwa people, they still take their skin group, and consequently their moiety, from their relationship to their mother. This means they will be opposite moiety to the mother, even though this also involves being of opposite moiety to their father. This deviation from the norm shows the primary structuring rule is the relationship between the mother and child, rather than that between the father and child.

The other way in which the two circles of skin groups are joined is through a reciprocal relationship between 'owners', called gidjan, and 'custodians', called junggayi. Each skin group has a primary custodial relationship, called first-choice junggayi, to another skin group that is of the opposite skin group circle. This involves reciprocal rights and responsibilities, since all people are owners of some tracts of land and particular ceremonies and custodians of others. In ceremonies the first preference will be for men of Wamut skin group to paint designs on men of Gotjok skin group and vice versa. At the more general level of moiety, Yirritja people will be the 'workers' in ceremonies, such as the *Gunapippi*, that are owned by Dhuwa people and Dhuwa people will be the workers in ceremonies, such as *Jabuduruwa*, that are owned by Yirritja people. This builds flexibility into the system and ensures that ceremonies and land are cared for properly even if people of the preferred skin group were not available. Ultimately, all Dhuwa people are custodians for all Yirritja people and all Yirritja people are custodians for all Dhuwa people.

It is no coincidence that a person's first-choice jungayyi is the classificatory brother or sister of their first-choice wife or husband. The classificatory brother or sister of their second-choice partner is the second-choice junggayi, while the third- and fourth-choice jungayyi will be of the opposite moiety but within the same skin group circle. These arrangements tie particular families closely to

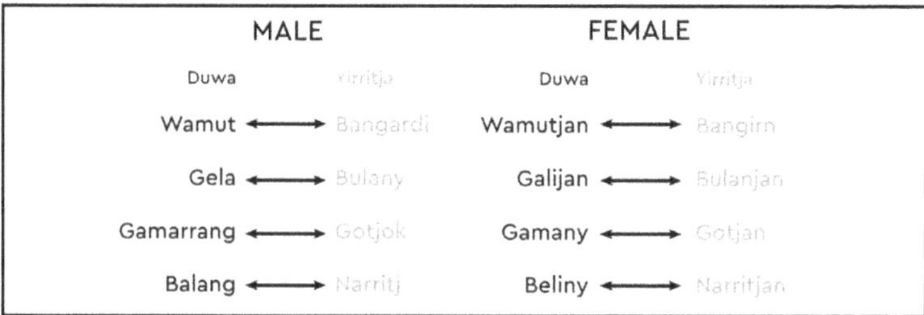

Figure 1.5

First choice junggayi relationships for Ngalkpon people

each other and create a situation in which all people have especially close family and ceremonial ties to others.

It was into this complex and sophisticated social system that British colonisation intruded. Not knowing the languages, not willing to learn them and secure in their belief that any people that did not have an ostensible material culture must be either savages or children of nature, the first non-Aboriginal colonisers of this region had no idea of the social complexity of the groups with whom they were interacting and would remain ignorant of this complexity for many decades.

First Contact

British colonisation radically disrupted the lives of Aboriginal people in the Barunga–Wugularr region, as it did everywhere on the Australian continent. It introduced a barrage of foreign concepts, beliefs, attitudes and diseases; it changed the physical landscape, destroyed languages, fragmented groups and separated families. Although it happened at different times in different parts of Australia, the lifestyles of all of Australia's Indigenous peoples were affected in similar and often devastating ways.

The British occupation of Australia was based on the notion of *terra nullius* (land with no people) which assumed that the land was effectively without owners. This view was accepted because the Aboriginal system of land ownership was not understood by Europeans and because to Europeans the natural resources of the land did not seem to be effectively exploited or managed by Aboriginal people. The doctrine of *terra nullius* was based on the assumption that Aboriginal social organisation was not sufficiently developed for Aboriginal people to possess rights over and interests in their land.

This doctrine underpinned the legal basis for the British acquisition of Australian land and was, under the British legal system, the foundation for extinguishing Indigenous title to land. From the British point of view, settlement became sovereignty. It took a long time, however, for Indigenous people in the various parts of Australia to understand that the European colonisers felt they owned the land that Aboriginal people had inherited through their forebears. For people in the Barunga–Wugularr region, extended contact with European Australians did not occur until the 1930s and '40s, and for many people it was not until this time that the notion dawned on them that somebody else felt they owned the land that Aboriginal people had inherited under ancestral laws.

The first contacts Aboriginal people in the Barunga–Wugularr region had with Europeans were with explorers. Leichardt's expedition of 1844–45, which followed Flying Fox Creek to the South Alligator River, would have traversed land belonging to Rembarrnga and, possibly, Ngalkpon people. The Gregory expedition of 1855–56 came closer to Barunga territory since it passed through southern sections of Jawoyn lands while en route from the Victoria River to the Roper. Not all of these encounters were friendly, and Alfred Giles, while travelling to what is now Katherine in 1871 recorded an assault on his camp by Aboriginal people in the Roper river area:

> Three natives have just come up bringing five other young men with them whom we have not before seen they gave us to understand that they had been a long way to find them to look at us. This however only strengthens my belief that they fully intend attempting attack upon us . . . I shall keep a sharp lookout tonight for the rascals.[6]

Giles' party fired upon the group of Aboriginal men, forcing them back and Giles later recovered bundles of spears which he assumed had been abandoned as the men fled.

The Overland Telegraph Line linking Adelaide and Darwin was built between 1870 and 1872 and virtually followed the route marked out by McDouall Stuart. The building of this line involved the establishment of semi-permanent encampments for workers, camps which attracted large numbers of Aboriginal people from the region who were quick to incorporate into their own economies the new material goods, such as iron, leather and tin, that had become available to them. McDouall Stuart's expedition of 1862 and Lindsay's of 1883 also appear to have come within the immediate vicinity of what is now Barunga. McDouall Stuart's reports of the agricultural and pastoral potential of the region north of the Roper River were among the factors that in 1863 prompted the annexation of the Northern Territory by South Australia.

Cattle and Conflict

It was only with the coming of cattle, however, that European colonisation became a reality for many Aboriginal people. The first pastoral lease to include the country around Barunga and Wugularr was taken up in 1881 by Fisher, Lyons and Co., though intensive pastoral activity did not occur in this region until early in the twentieth century. The expansion of the pastoral industry went hand-in-hand with war between Aboriginal and non-Aboriginal people. Given the disparity in the effectiveness of their weapons, the consequences for Aboriginal people were calamitous.

The Aboriginal population in all parts of Australia declined sharply in the decades following white settlement. Population estimates for the country as a whole prior to European colonisation range from around 300,000, by Radcliffe-Brown in 1930,[7] to approximately one million, by Butlin in 1983,[8] with the latter now being the more generally accepted figure.[9] The differences in these estimates are important because they illustrate (or give emphasis to) particular views in the past. The traditional view of historians is that of a small black population that made little impact on the natural environment and which largely 'faded away' before the superior forces of white colonisation. The converse view is of a much more substantial and active Indigenous population that consciously manipulated the resources in their environment and which engaged in warfare against white colonisers. By 1921 the official estimate of the Aboriginal populations was around 60,000.[10] This decline in population can be attributed to the effects of introduced diseases, such as smallpox and tuberculosis, and to the deliberate and extended violence that was an integral component of white colonisation strategies.[11]

In the Victoria River District, about 300 kilometres east of Barunga, Rose[12] estimates that the Aboriginal population decreased from around 4000–5000 in 1883 to 187 in 1939, when the first census was prepared by the Victoria River District Station. Her estimate of a population depleted by up to 95 per cent is comparable to that of Keen[13] who suggests that population loss in the Alligator River region was around 97 per cent, as well as the figures collected by Mulvaney[14] for the Alice Springs area. Rose states that:

> . . . the process of establishing cattle stations was the one which had the most profound impact on Aboriginal people. Most of the managers and workers came from Queensland where they had apparently developed strategies through which the country could efficiently be made safe for their purposes. It seems that the initial tactic was to kill; after this period of ruthless extermination, the second tactic was to incorporate the survivors into the station work force.[15]

Population losses of this order support the argument that the white colonisation of Australia was based on a deliberate practice of genocide, since it would appear that the intention, either premeditated or not, was to bring about the destruction of a group of people. While the question of genocide has not been well articulated in Australian histories, it has been the subject of research by Tony Barta16 and, more recently, Henry Reynolds.17 Barta argues that all white people in contemporary Australia have an implicit 'relationship of genocide' to all Aborigines, that in the 'key relation, the appropriation of the land, it is fundamental to the society in which they live'.18

Once Aboriginal people realised that European colonisation was dependent on the success of pastoralism, they adopted a strategy of cattle killing and expelling cattle from Aboriginal traditional lands. The repercussions, however, were tragic. One of the members of the Territory's South Australian parliament commented that:

> I know of one station where the natives killed fifty or sixty cattle in one lot. The squatters would not mind them killing a beast now and then for food, and in fact they often give the natives a beast for food. It was simply wanton destruction, and they not only speared fifty or sixty head of cattle, but they drove hundreds of them off the country altogether in the glorious cattle hunt of theirs. I believe in this case that the station owners went out and met the very tribe who had done the damage, and caught them red-handed with portions of meat with them. They gave them a lesson – 'dispersed' them I think is the term used in official reports – and the natives have been very much quieter in that district, and have given very little trouble since that day.[19]

This statement makes it clear that while the police and pastorialists may have been the ones to implement these actions they involved the compliance of the general public as well as the government of the day. As Mulvaney[20] states, 'Police 'dispersion' related essentially to hunting cattle killers. It was human lives for bullocks'.

It is a measure of the strength of the prevailing social views that some of these incidents were documented in the newspapers of the time. For example, a letter to the editor published in the *Northern Territory Times and Gazette* on 11th July 1885 estimates that 'not less than 150 Aboriginals, a great part of these women and children' were killed in retribution for the murder by Aboriginals of four settlers on the Daly River. The editorial column of the same paper on the 4th October 1884 discussed the murder of several copper miners by Aboriginal people:

> Backwards the natives must move before the tide of civilization, or, if they will not give place peaceably, and show their natures are as dangerous as the venomous serpent, even as every man will crush a snake under his heel, so must the hand of every man be raised against a tribe of inhuman monsters, whose cowardly and murderous nature renders them unfit to live.

Sentiments such as these underpinned retributive raids on Aboriginal groups. Such sentiments sprung from the notion that Aboriginal people were on a lower level of the evolutionary scale and, in any case, were doomed to extinction. These views agreed with the contemporary theory of social Darwinism, in which social development was perceived as being analogous to biological evolution. The reasoning advanced was that the stronger 'race' was destined to subdue weaker 'races', thereby ensuring the survival of the fittest. In southern Australia, this view is expressed in an 1888 editorial in the *Melbourne Age*:

> It seems a law of nature that where two races whose stages of progression differ greatly are brought into contact, the inferior race is doomed to wither and disappear.[21]

The southern view is considerably less harsh than that expressed in the northern newspapers of the times, reflecting the relative distance of their readers from the colonial frontier. As Goodwin[22] points out, the doctrine of social evolution in its cruder forms was 'particularly attractive to successful members of the business and pastoral community and to all advocates of rugged individualism'. Such opinions were actively endorsed and ratified by anthropologists until well into the middle of the twentieth century. In 1891 A.W. Howitt presented an early and explicit formulation of this view:

> The aborigines in all parts of Australia where settlement is in progress are more or less rapidly dying out, and even where this is least apparent, the contact of the white man destroys the primitive structure of their society, and modifies their beliefs. Indeed, in all parts of Australia the native race is doomed to destruction sooner or later, contact with the white race is fatal; the aborigines lose the original savage virtue, and acquire our vices which destroy them.[23]

There were many violent incidents throughout Australia which, taken together, constituted a series of undeclared wars between black and white Australians. In the Barunga–Wugularr region, this involved killing as well as the kidnapping of women, as described by George Jaurdaku:

> Before I was born in this country there were a lot of people here. People were shooting people. This lot here, whitefellas used to chase them along and shoot them.
>
> You know that airstrip there? That's the place they were shooting people. The wild blackfellas. They had nothing, no English, no tucker. We only knew bush tucker. Bush blackfella. They speared white man too. They killed a big mob up here at this spring. My old Granpa, his name was old Snowball, he belonged to this country. He was shot right here [shows the cheek place where the shot went in and where it came out]. And that Kenneth Murray's grandpa. Larry and Dick's father, they shot him. They shot him in this country poorfella. This river here.
>
> . . . They [the policemen] had chained up one old lady and they'd taken her. One bloke whose name was Wak-Wak, that was his missus they'd chained up. She was singing out all the way. They had a chain on her and she walked all the way singing out,
>
> 'Help. Come on. Help me-e. I'm here. Where are you?'
>
> They never answered. They just sat down there and waited in the jungle scrub.
>
> The police were coming up, all the way up. As they were going past, the spear was thrown, shovel spear. The police got out their revolver and fired a shot. He's dead, that policeman.
>
> They grabbed that old girl. They took her away. They kilim [hit] that chain. They broke it up.

> They buried him, that policeman, out in the bush. They couldn't take him back. Too far, and there was the biggest scrub. Salt water place. Blue Mud Bay, that's the place.[24]

Women were a source of friction between Aboriginal and European men. There were few European women on the colonial frontier. European men regularly had liaisons with Aboriginal women, but did not understand, or were not willing to abide by Aboriginal rules. In some cases arguments over women erupted into violence and even murder. Jimmy Wesan describes such a circumstance:

> That *mununga* [whitefella] he didn't want blackfellas, only Aboriginal girl. He used to keep them girls and that right people [husbands] for their wives, they got nothing. So them blackfellas get wild, kill 'em, get rid of them mununga. My grandfather been working at Mainoru. That *mununga* used to rob him of his wife, that old Bobby. This old man and old Dick, my uncle, and 'long leg', they called him Bangardi. Those two old men tell Bobby 'you tell us what time we got to take that *mununga* bush. We take that *mununga* la bush and kill him.'
>
> They been go longa that country *waaruk ngaluk*, Dingo Dreaming, That Bobby been say to that *mununga*. 'You go and make a short hobble for that horse'. Those two men were hiding la bush, those two murdering blokes. That *mununga* was going to take the hobble off. He tried to bend down and they speared him. Long shovel spear. Him sing out 'leave me alone.' Another spear hit him in the right place. Then they got a big stick, hit him on the head, drop him. Those fellas been cut him, make him into quarters, cut off his head. Hung him up like kangaroo, quarter, in the tree, so that crow or anything can eat him. Half on the ground for the dingo, half in the tree for the crow.
>
> They been cruel. They been cut this one [pointing to genital area] and take it back to them girls. 'You mob can take this one, keep him in your dilly bag till him dry. Then you can throw it away, or give it to the dog. You don't do this you going to go the same way as this *mununga*.' They been do that. The other Aboriginal girls been frightened to go with *mununga* then. They might get [the] same thing. This happened long time ago.[25]

Jimmy Wesan's account shows that this particular murder served two purposes: the elimination of the person who was taking their wives and as a cautionary tale for other Aboriginal women. Occasionally, it also happened that Aboriginal people abducted

European women. Sometimes these women lived out their lives in the communities into which they had been brought:

> They took one white lady away. They said, 'You're not going to go. You've got to stop with us. You can't go back to mother or father for one year.'
>
> The kept her there at Blue Mud Bay. She couldn't talk. She talked only English. They gave her bush tucker, goanna, wallaby, fish, turtle, everything. They had a lot of sons and that old woman died in the bush. My father told me.[26]

It is difficult to assess whether the Barunga–Wugularr region was subject to the same level of violence as in other parts of the Northern Territory. Those who lived in central Arnhem Land would have been protected to a certain extent from the aggression of pastoralists, but those around the location of Barunga itself would have been more vulnerable, especially during the time that it was a pastoral property. George Jaurdaku, for example, was shot when stealing cattle:

> I was shot by one boss. Alec McDonald shot me for poddy dodging. We used to break into the yard in the night and take away cattle to make a lot of cattle in Roper Valley. I stayed out in the bush for two years. Then I went to hospital. I got the lead here, under the skin.[27]

The most notorious incident in the Barunga–Wugularr region, however, occurred when the manager of Mainoru station, Tom Boddington, poisoned the rations given to Aboriginal stockmen and their families. Daisy Borduk's recollection of this shows an innocent bewilderment:

> Boddington, he poisoned all the people at Mainoru. They worked for him but . . . I don't know what he meant [why he did it]. When they started to fall down . . . they knew he'd poisoned that tucker. That man, now, Boddington. And they ate that [special] mud and . . . got mud and vomit, [to try to] get up that poison. Then they came here to Beswick . . . He gave it to all the stockmen and their wives and kids, too . . . The policeman came . . . they were Rembarrnga and Ngalkpon tribe. He was a bad man that Boddington . . . They made damper but it was no good, it had poison, he poisoned them. And when they ate it they gave some to their dogs and the ants, like these bull ants, all died. They held their dogs [upside down] by two legs and they vomited . . . They tried it

> out on those ants, second time. First time, they did not savvy [understand] . . . He was a tricky fellow, he tricked them . . . two times.[28]

Bandicoot Robinson was Boddington's off-sider at the time of the poisoning and his account suggests that this incident was related to a feud between Boddington and Billy Farrer, rather than the simple victimisation of Aboriginal people. Boddington had replaced Farrer as manager of Mainoru station, but Farrer appears to have had this overturned. Boddington had retaliated as he left the station:

> I was working for him, now, Tom Boddington. He was a bad bloke, too. He used to shoot, frighten the hell out of all those people . . . Before we left he put all that arsenic, poison. He poisoned the salt, he poisoned the sugar, he poisoned the tea leaf, that box full of tea leaf. He poisoned all that . . . Old Billy Farrer was loading all the boys on that buggy, two buggies. He took them right up to Katherine hospital. Tom Boddington told me 'You know that Mainoru mob. I sang them that song. They're all here at hospital. Or maybe they're all dead now'.[29]

The official documentation of this incident indicates the manner in which white administrators massaged their records to conceal these kinds of offences, masking which occurred in many parts of Australia.30 The most explicit references to the Mainoru poisioning that occur in the Katherine police journal[31] for June 1940 are to 'investigations re sick natives from Mainoru', the matter of 'Farrer v. Boddington' and feeding 'witness Bandicoot' over an extended period.

This administrative veiling of European violence against Indigenous peoples was normal procedure during the early years of white settlement in northern Australia. The lives of Aboriginal people were not thought to be valuable. This view was reinforced by a conspiracy of silence among Europeans living and working in these areas. European administrators intentionally masked the violence inflicted on Aboriginal groups, indirectly contributing to the near genocide of these groups. From the point of view of individual administrators, such masking prevented interference from southerners and facilitated the autonomous administration of the Northern Territory. From a more general perspective, however, it can be seen to facilitate the myth of a relatively uncontested and peaceful settlement in the northern outreaches of Australia – indeed of Australia as a whole – and the 'success story' of white colonisation, important factors in construction of the Australian national identity.

Two

Surviving Protection

The point I tried to make in my earlier remarks was that if we leave the aborigines in the north alone they will die out. On the other hand, if we bring them under our influence they will breed, and their numbers increase until they menace our security.

Dr Cook, the Protector of Aborigines for the Northern Territory at the 1937 Conference of Chief Protectors.

Protectionism

In the Northern Territory the official response to the violence of pastoralists and a perceived need to control Aboriginal people was the policy of protectionism, embodied in the passage of the *Aboriginals Ordinance*, 1918–1947. The ordinance aimed to provide for the moral and physical protection of Aboriginal people and was based on the assumption that Aboriginal people were a dying race and that the best thing that could be done by European Australians was to 'smooth the dying pillow'.[1] One of the early proponents of this view was Daisy Bates:

> The simple fact is that in this meeting of extremes – ultra civilization and primitive man – the latter must disappear ... It cannot be too much stressed that the Aborigines are a dying race, and the only thing that can be done for them is to make their passing easier.[2]

The ordinance also aimed to control the movements of Aboriginal people but, in its early stages it did not particularly focus on controlling Aboriginal culture. In this sense, it ushered in a 'softer' phase than the later period of assimilation.

The *Aboriginals Ordinance* and its amendments were the principal legislation to affect Aboriginal people in the Northern Territory during the first half of the twentieth century. It established a Chief Protector of Aboriginals, appointed by the Administrator of the Northern Territory, whose duty it was to 'exercise a general supervision and care over all matters affecting the welfare of Aboriginals and to protect them against immorality, injustice, imposition and fraud'. The ordinance was administered by Protectors – and in the early days, all policemen were Protectors also – and by selected officials of the Native Affairs Branch. The European community at that time was generally agreed that it was in the best interests of Aboriginals.[3]

The ordinance focused on controlling the property and physical movement of Aboriginal people and on structuring the type of contact that could occur between Aboriginals and non-Aboriginals. Among other things, the provisions of this ordinance gave the Chief Protector the power to:

- Declare any area to be a prohibited area for Aboriginals.
- Receive or dispose of any property, real or personal, owned by any Aboriginal or half-caste.
- Decide whether or not marriage between an Aboriginal woman and a non–Aboriginal man should be allowed.
- Remove an Aboriginal from a Reserve or from one Reserve to another, unless the Aboriginal was lawfully employed, held a permit to be absent from the Reserve or was a woman married to a person substantially of European descent for whom, in the opinion of the Chief Protector, satisfactory provision had been made.
- Take an Aboriginal or half-caste into custody if, in his opinion, it was necessary or desirable in the interests of the Aboriginal or half-caste for him to do so and for that purpose could enter any premises where the Aboriginal or half-caste was likely to be found.
- Issue a Licence to Employ Aboriginals.

The ordinance was based on three main assumptions:

- European customs and systems were inherently superior to those of Aboriginal people.
- Aboriginal people were not able to ensure their own moral and physical welfare.
- Aboriginal people were unable to protect themselves from exploitation by non-Aboriginals.

Subsequently, all of these assumptions have been proven wrong. They are based on a conception of Aboriginal people as passive recipients of government policy or respondents to the actions of Europeans, rather than as agents active in creating and shaping their own lives, both as individuals and as cohesive groups. It is ironic, however, that beneath this lay the further assumption that the smooth running of European society depended on the actions of the Aboriginal people who were being 'controlled'.

The details of the *Aboriginals Ordinance* 1918–1947 reflect the concerns of the wider public at the time. Europeans were affronted, and probably threatened, by the prospect of uncontrolled actions of drunken Aboriginal people and so the ordinance prohibited Aboriginal people from drinking alcohol or from being employed on licensed premises. At a time immediately following the brutality of first contact and invasion, Europeans wanted to minimise any violence from Aboriginal people and so the ordinance prohibited Aboriginal people from possessing or carrying a firearm without a license. Aboriginal people today, however, comment that from their point of view – and given the history of the area – it would have been better if the ordinance had prohibited *non*-Aboriginal people from possessing or carrying a firearm without a license.

The over-riding preoccupation of Europeans was with preventing cross-cultural liaisons, and the birth of children of mixed parentage. This is apparent in the many provisions of the ordinance relating to the removal of children of mixed descent as well as in the prohibition against Aboriginal women being employed by anyone of 'Asiatic or Negro race' (who were themselves suspect because of their non-European heritage) and the provision that Aboriginal women were not allowed to cohabit with non-Aboriginal men. It is also notable that while marriage between a female Aboriginal and a European male could only be obtained with the permission of the Chief Protector of Aboriginals, the idea of marriage between a European woman and an Aboriginal man was never mooted.

The *Aboriginals Ordinance* of 1936 made it an offence for a European man to live, cohabit or have sexual intercourse with any 'Aboriginal or half-caste to whom he was not lawfully married'. The penalty was £100, six months in prison or both. The enforcement of this law was a focus of both Police and Native Affairs Branch administration and much of the documentary correspondence of the period is directed towards this. Children of mixed descent were proof that this law had been broken so, apart from the implementation of direct instructions, it was in the interests of the relevant officials to facilitate the removal of the children to the various half-caste institutions within the Northern Territory.

Children from the Barunga–Wugularr region, none of whom spoke English at the time, were generally sent to the Croker Island Half-Caste Institution. The preferred age of removal was around four years while there was still considered to be some hope of 'moulding' the children.[4] As discussed in Chapter Six, the effects of this policy on both the children and their families were calamitous.

The provisions of the 1936 ordinance were rooted in a concern to consolidate the European colonisation of the Northern Territory. For instance, the initial conference of Commonwealth and State Aboriginal Authorities held in Canberra during April, 1937, resolved:

> DESTINY OF THE RACE
> that this Conference believes that the destiny of the natives of aboriginal origin, but not of the full blood, lies in their ultimate absorption by the people of the Commonwealth, and it therefore recommends that all efforts be directed to that end.

However, the implementation of an assimilation policy was marred by contradictions, one of the most striking being that the methods used actually achieved segregation rather than assimilation. This policy can best be understood in terms of the concern of the Territory administration with controlling the movements of Aboriginal people.

The Northern Territory administration was obsessed with controlling the movements of Aboriginal people. In part, this served to minimise the embarrassment caused by their sub-standard living conditions, the solution seen as most appropriate being to establish Aboriginal settlements at a distance from townships where their living conditions were out of sight, out of mind. For instance, the conditions at Tandangal, as described later in this chapter, would not have been tolerated to the same extent if the settlement had been close to a major township.

Paradoxically, during this period of ostensible 'protection' there was little tangible help available to Aboriginal people. In the Barunga–Wugularr region the main support in this respect were the Aged and Infirm Depots established at Mataranka, Katherine and Pine Creek. These depots distributed rations and blankets and provided treatment for Aboriginals who were sick with serious contagious diseases such as leprosy.[5] Auxiliary ration depots were also established temporarily in areas of the Northern Territory experiencing periods of extended drought. In 1930 W.B. Kirkland, the Chief Protector of Aboriginals, expressed a concern that these depots:

> . . . encourage the native to become lazy, dependent and eventually unfit to hunt for himself, and tend to destroy the tribal life.[6]

This comment is interesting not only because it indicates the autonomy in the daily lives of many Aboriginal people at that time – they were providing their own food and shelter – but also because it implies an acceptance by Europeans of, and even a respect for, 'tribal life'. This is the principle difference between the relatively benign and exclusionist policies of protectionism and the later, more destructive and actively interventionist policies of assimilation.

Mining at Maranboy

Because protectionist policies were concerned primarily with maintaining physical distance between Aboriginal and non-Aboriginal people, they had no great effect on Aboriginal people living in remote areas such as Arnhem Land. In the Barunga–Wugularr region, only about 80 kilometres (50 miles) from the township of Katherine, extended contact between Europeans and Aboriginal people had its beginnings in 1913 when tin was found at Maranboy by two prospectors, Tom Richardson and James Sharber. The area was proclaimed a goldfield later that same year. In January 1916, the establishment of a Government Battery, with crushing facilities to make the mining of low-grade ore viable,[7] signalled the whites' intention to stay. Louis Stuttard was appointed manager of the battery and remained at Maranboy until his retirement in 1944.[8]

A police station was established in close proximity to the Maranboy mines almost immediately they were established. It served a similar function to the Aged and Infirm Depots in the townships and also acted as a point of first contact for primary Aboriginal health care. Many diseases were rife, the most common being malaria, tuberculosis, berri berri, sexually transmitted diseases and leprosy. There are regular references to 'sick abos' in the Maranboy Police Journals of the period. Aboriginals with leprosy

Figure 2.1
The remains of Maranboy Government Battery

were permanently removed to leprosariums in the north. An Australian Inland Mission (AIM) hospital opened in 1917 in response to an outbreak of malaria and berri berri among the non-Aboriginal community.[9] However, the hospital was not open to Aboriginal people on the grounds that if Aboriginals used it, Europeans would not.[10]

The Maranboy mines were amongst the most important in the Northern Territory for many decades. In the year 1938–39 for instance, 21 tons of concentrates, valued at £3,277, were produced, while the next most productive mines at Anningie and Coniston yielded only four tons, valued at £665.[11] The Maranboy mines were productive until the mid-1950s, after which they became increasingly idle. They were finally closed down in 1965 when the remnant plant equipment, buildings and scrap was sold.[12]

The establishment of the Maranboy tin field resulted in extended contact of an unprecedented nature between Aboriginal groups from the southern Arnhem Land area. The movement of Aboriginals to the field precipitated a more sedentary lifestyle than that experienced pre-contact and, for many, provided the first experiences of extended contact with Europeans. Traditional hunting and foraging patterns were disrupted and elders today comment that the introduction of flour and sugar was the main disruption to their economy. Prior to this, the daily lives of Aboriginal people had held few of the stresses that characterised European existence at that time. Jimmy Wesan describes his life as a child during this period:

> They sit down one day only. If him really good place, might sit down two days. Find everything, fish, kangaroo, bush tucker. My father used to kill two kangaroos or three. We used to stay for two days and go on. Other times one day, one day, one day, all the way. Only ceremony time might be stay in one place three or four months. Hunting all over the place, kill kangaroo or bush tucker, yam, or lily, water lily, cheeky yam, any sort of tucker.[13]

The changes in settlement patterns that occurred at this time also caused a realignment of relations between Aboriginal language groups and a growth in the religious ties of non-Jawoyn people to the Maranboy area. These were intensified when the next generation was conceived, giving them special birthrights and responsibilities to the land in that area.

A number of the senior people now living at Barunga, including Peter Manabaru of the Ngalkpon language group, were born at Maranboy, and many of their own children were born at Barunga. Children born at Maranboy from non-Jawoyn language groups would have been among the first Aboriginal people born in country truly remote from that to which they had inherited affiliations. An occurrence of this phenomenon in pre-contact history would have been unusual and perhaps only related to attendance at ceremonies in distant areas.

The concentrations of Aboriginals in the Maranboy area raised the issue of the establishment of a reserve in the area. The Maranboy Common was reserved in May 1920, and in April 1923 a six-acre (2.43 ha) Aboriginal reserve was declared at the request of Police Constable Harold Giles,[14] who at that time had primary administrative responsibility for Aboriginal people in the area. Giles later applied for the position of manager of Beswick station.

As with many other Australian pioneer ventures,[15] Aboriginal labour was essential to the economic viability of the Maranboy mining fields and in 1919 the permanent Aboriginal population there numbered thirty. Harlow[16] notes that the proclamation of the Maranboy field under the *Goldfields Amendment* Act of 1886 – which prevented Asians from mining on any field discovered by a

European for a period of two years – and the renewal of this proclamation every two years, effectively prevented Chinese from mining the area. This made the Maranboy field unusual when compared to most other mining fields in the Northern Territory at that time and led to European miners at Maranboy becoming particularly reliant on both male and female Aboriginal labour.

According to O'Reilly,[17] a miner at Maranboy in its early days, miners had to pay 10 shillings a week – less than £22 per year – to the Acting Protector for each Aboriginal for whom he held a permit to employ. This fee was augmented by payment in kind. In 1943, a year after the mine had produced tin concentrate valued at £8,000, the miners claimed that it cost them 'roughly about £100 per year to feed and clothe one Boy'. It is likely that this estimate was inflated since the standard of living attainable by Aboriginal people was not high. Daisy Borduk[18] recalled that workers at Maranboy were paid 5 shillings a week, plus flour – the women made dresses of the flourbags – tea, sugar, half a block of tobacco, and clothes. They had no houses, only bough shelters, and in the wet season they slept in rock shelters. At this time there were 24 Aboriginal men and their families living on a reasonably permanent basis at Maranboy.

As in many other parts of Australia, Aboriginal people during this period were disempowered through not being given cash payment for their work. Any wages they did earn were deposited in the Aboriginal Benefits Trust Fund once all amounts spent 'on behalf of or for the benefit of the Aborigine' had been deducted. An important point here is that the idea of what constituted 'benefit' was decided by white administrators, rather than by Aboriginal people themselves. In practice, it was extremely difficult and often impossible for Aboriginal people to get access to these funds as the money could only be spent with authorisation from the Chief Protector, located in Darwin. This was a continual source of annoyance and frustration for Aboriginal people who rightly regarded it as unjust and discriminatory. The practice is a prime example of the structural racism integral to the framework of the administrative systems created by Europeans to control and disempower Aboriginals.

Aboriginal men and women alike were engaged not only in the mining operations but in a range of other tasks including bread-making, wood-cutting, locating mineral deposits and carting of goods. Additionally Aboriginal women worked as domestics for miners, local officials and their families. The mother of Phyllis Wiynjorroc worked in this capacity for Stuttard, the manager of the Government Battery at Maranboy, and also at the police station, while Peter Manabaru's father worked as a police tracker.

Figure 2.2
Maudie Weston and police trackers,
including George Weston, big brother of Jimmy Wesan, 1940
Australian Archives (ACT)
CRS M119/3 113

Legislation passed in 1945, restricting the employment of Aboriginals in underground mining,[19] was met with opposition from the Maranboy miners, who are reported as claiming that the order was 'tantamount to excluding native labour from the field altogether, as they [the miners] were not prepared to work below surface themselves with a native operating the winch'.[20]

Aboriginal people were attracted to the Maranboy field for a variety of reasons. Curiosity was often the main reason that they came, and access to European goods and technology the main reason they stayed. An interview with Spider Brennan gives some indication of the freedom to choose between the benefits of the bush and those of Maranboy that Aboriginal people had at this time:

Look that mine,

Oh, I bin work little while, and I go back longa my daddy and my mother, to bush.

And we bin sit down, might be, one year. Missing tobacco again. He tobacco in Maranboy.

Oh, might be I go back again. Back again, yeah, Maranboy.

. . . Yeah, oh like it, tobacco and tea, like that, you know, because bush, sometimes I get [no] breakfast, sometimes three day no tucker, in the bush, that's why I bin thinking,

'Oh, I have to go back again Maranboy.'

Every day that breakfast tucker! Every day that dinner time tucker.

Right, we bin stay here altogether.[21]

During this period Aboriginal cultural life appears to have continued without major modification. In this respect, people in the Barunga–Wugularr region were fortunate that the settlement was not a mission aiming to replace Indigenous belief systems with Christianity; working at the mines did not unduly interrupt Aboriginal ceremonial activity. Shafts would regularly flood during the wet season making it virtually impossible to work underground and Aboriginal people tended to resume a pre-contact lifestyle during this time of the year. Henrietta Pearce, wife of one of the Maranboy miners, recalls meeting a group of Aboriginal men with painted bodies, whom she described as 'callers in warpaint', returning from a ceremony near Beswick Creek.[22] O'Reilly saw many such ceremonies:

> In the evenings around their campfires, after filling their elastic stomachs with the whitefellows' tucker, they amused themselves by corroborreeing the events of the day. Every action of their white bosses would be depicted in pantomime . . . They often held native corroborees, which generally are in the form of dances barred to whites.[23]

Peter Manabaru recalls learning from his grandfather how to make rock art and bark paintings at around this time:

> Sometime him say I'm gonna show you longa stone. Drawing. Longa cave inside. Might be him say 'I'm gona put this Mimi drawing, so you put him like that and you paint him, another one. Sometime Mimi him killem kangaroo, or sometime Mimi come along and killem that emu and sometime take him back home, emu or kangaroo . . . him [my grandfather] say you gada paint him with this one, this glue, that

> red glue with gum . . . might be him say 'you should know that one I bin show you'.[24]'

The settlement at Maranboy, however, had the potential to become a centre for cross-cultural conflict. Firstly, it was a major focus for the implementation of government policies aimed at controlling the movements and social interactions of Aboriginal people. Secondly, it was host to large encampments of Aboriginals who stayed for lengths of time no doubt unprecedented in Indigenous history. In retrospect, it is surprising that greater conflict has not been recorded for this period.

In some cases Aboriginal people moved to Maranboy to avoid the violence on the pastoral properties. Phyllis Wiynjorroc, for example, was told by her parents of Aboriginals moving to Maranboy from the Waterhouse area to avoid being killed on pastoral properties in that region. These fears were not imaginary: such killings were widespread throughout the Northern Territory at this time.[25]

This aggression was not uni-directional, and at least one miner at Maranboy was killed by Aboriginal people,[26] such actions seemingly taken after much provocation. The general store at Maranboy was run by Jack Shuter, a man with a reputation for violence, who is thought to have shot Aboriginal people. On one occasion Daisy Borduk's father and a friend raided Shuter's shop. They tied Shuter up, put his shotgun on the roof so he couldn't shoot them, and took what goods they needed – matches, corned beef, tobacco, flour, sugar and tea. Collecting their wives and children, they left for Dook Creek, near Beswick station, not returning to Maranboy until after Jack Shuter had left.[27]

The continued operation of the mines was dependent on Aboriginal labour, since most of the work was done by them. Magnolia Rankin remembers:

> George Fisher, long time him siddown. He bin one Aboriginal girlfriend, she bin die now. Him good man, tin mining boss. That's true. Blackfella do the work, not mununga.[28]

There were never large numbers of Europeans living at Maranboy: in 1942, for example, there were seven European miners and 24 Aboriginal men and their families. This dependence on Aboriginal labour meant that the miners had no choice but to adjust their operations to suit Aboriginal notions of work. O'Reilly[29] comments that this was done through allocating jobs, rather than hours. That this was actually articulated by the miners indicates that Aboriginal people had a degree of power over their situation and over the miners as well.

A serious incident occurred when the Native Affairs Branch decided to reduce undesirable contacts between miners and Aboriginal women by moving all of the latter from the mining area to the compound at Joe's Garden. This caused Aboriginal men to leave the field and, until the decision was reversed, the mine was in danger of closing down. The miners acted swiftly to ensure their continued economic viability and Stuttard, the manager of the battery, immediately sent a telegram to the Director of Mines in which he stated that productivity had practically ceased and pleaded for 'working aboriginals' to be allowed to retain their families on the mines. The miners also sent a letter to the Controller of Base Metals in which they stated that:

> The men called their working Boys and explained the position quietly to them. They appeared to be a bit bewildered, and passed no comment on the subject for a day or so. They apparently have no illusions about the matter now, for they informed us today, that if their womenfolk and families are going, they are going too.[30]

In response the Director of Mines informed the Administrator of the Northern Territory that:

> It has been generally accepted that were the employment of Aboriginal labour on the Maranboy tin field abolished it would result in the general closing down of all producing mines. Even with tin at the highest price it has never been possible for producers to develop these mines on such a scale as would warrant and support the employment of European labour and as premised, unless aboriginal labour can be employed by the operators, without doubt the field will be abandoned.[31]

It was during this period that a community comprising more than just members of the same language group began to emerge. It was the first time that different language groups from the wider region lived together for an extended period and must have caused adjustments in social relations between them. This appears to have occurred peaceably, as there is no indications of major friction between these groups in the documentation or oral histories of the time. However, this was also a period of considerable transition during which language groups other than the Jawoyn began to take responsibility for caring for this part of Jawoyn land.

Working for the Army

The next major contact that Barunga people had with European society took place during World War II, and their cooperation was again essential to the success of a primarily European endeavour. The Japanese bombed Darwin on the 19th February 1942 and Katherine on the 3rd and 22nd of March, prompting emergency wartime measures. From early March 1942 the whole of the Northern Territory north of Alice Springs was placed under military control, with large numbers of people evacuated south from that time. In August, Aboriginal people were prohibited from remaining north of the Edith River and the Native Affairs Branch of the Northern Territory Administration was made responsible for the establishment and management of control camps near the townships of Mataranka and Katherine. This relocation brought Aboriginal peoples from different areas into unprecedented and prolonged contact with each other. At the Mataranka compound, this included contact with groups, such as the Tiwi people from Melville and Bathurst Islands, with whom mainland people had previously had very limited contact.

This was a time when some Aboriginal people were seeing white people for the first time, as described by Jimmy Wesan:

> Olden days, they used to call him soldier. Soldier come in, he used to frighten us. People used to go la bush 'cause the soldier coming. They been frightened for that bomb. I been born when him been new war. He chucked that bomb from Katherine to Mataranka. That soldier say 'You don't have [to be] frightened. We just want to look around your land.' Some old people didn't want it that way. They didn't want to look la white man. Frighten. They go away now, long way round. Bush. Might be Poison Creek, or the long way from Poison Creek, Bulman. That been frightened. That's the first time they been see that mununga [white person]. Army time.[32]

During the Second World War many Aboriginal people chose to leave the Arnhem Land Reserve, conducting ethnographic forays into a European economic system. Paddy Fordham Wainburranga recalls:

> When the war time came, when the war was being fought and the bombs were coming down, my mother and father told me: 'Hey! All your uncles, all the family have been gone a long time. To Maranboy. What about us going?' Well, I didn't know. Anyway, all the family, my father and his four wives, all my brothers and sisters walked down. It took us three or four weeks to get there. To the Territory. Maranboy.
>
> . . . I became a young man after the war and then I learnt about the white man. How the white man treated me. How he gave me clothes. Native Affairs government. They sent our people out of Arnhem Land . . . Rembarrnga people, Ngalkbun people. They all cleared out. All went to Katherine, or to Bamyili, or to Beswick station.[33]

The Defence Division in 1942 employed 177 Aboriginal people at Mataranka. Their conditions of employment were as follows: wages – 5 shillings per week; special work 10 s.; rations – 10 pounds. beef, 7 lbs flour, 14 ounces sugar, 3 oz. tea, 1 lb. jam, 3 lbs rice, 2 oz. tobacco per week; 1 lb. of baking powder to 50 lbs of flour; potatoes and onions when no rice available; clothing – 2 pairs drill trousers, 2 shirts, one blanket, one ground-sheet, one towel; mess gear – one each plate, mug, spoon, knife, fork.[34] These rations were intended to feed and clothe employee's families as well as themselves, and were the reason cited by the Administrator for the comparatively small wage. The Chief Inspector for the Inspector General of Administration noted that:

> The aboriginal is undoubtably strong, and could stand more continuous work in this climate than the average white man. In this town they are performing many useful tasks for civilian employers, and even if it were considered that two natives would be required to do one white man's work, the economic cost would still be less, while it is imperative that all latent labour should be exploited at present.[35]

Aboriginal people at Mataranka were employed by the Army in excavation and road work, maintenance of the railway track, cutting and collecting firewood, laundry and kitchen work, carting and stacking ammunition, motor assembly and dismantling, and other manual tasks. The work was allocated according to gender, which was consistent with both Aboriginal and non-Aboriginal social rules of the time.

Army policy and practice had a positive effect upon many Aboriginal people in the Northern Territory. Hall[36] points out that for

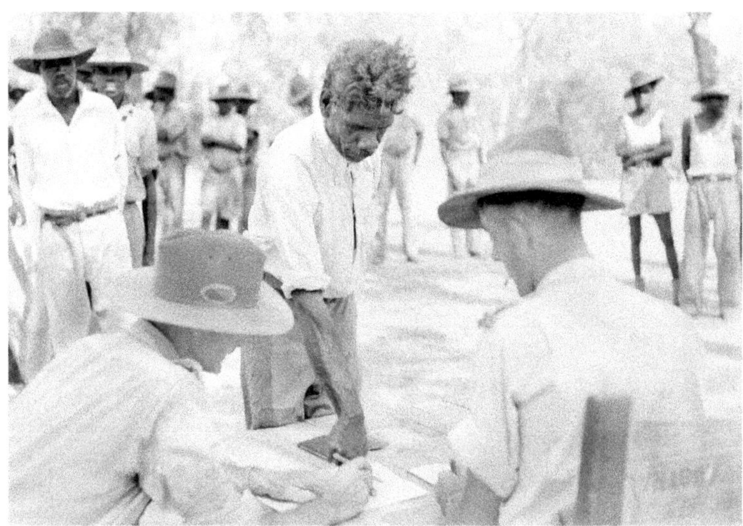

Figure 2.3
Aboriginal men lined up to collect their Army pay, Katherine, 1943
Australian War Memorial Negative Number 057362

Figure 2.4
Australian troops learning the 'secrets' of native bush craft
Australian War Memorial Negative Number 013578

Figure 2.5
Aboriginal stockman being handed a rifle to dispose of a rogue bullock
Australian War Memorial
Negative Number 014284

those who went into combat alongside Europeans the experience of sharing danger created highly cohesive bonds which left no room for racism or other divisive pressures. And this camaraderie was also felt by those who worked within Australia. Nellie Camfoo, now of Bulman, comments that:

> I been like to work with them army people, army ladies. Not only me you know. Thirty or forty young girls working on that army job. Some been die and some still alive at Barunga. Cooking, washing, ironing clothes. We always want to help. We fight la Japanese. Guns and knives.[37]

The war years presented an opportunity for Aboriginals to demonstrate that their relationships with whites could be something other than unremittingly hostile, as many Europeans had assumed.[38] These new relationships of order, cooperation and trust are depicted visually in Figures 2.3, 2.4 and 2.5. For many Aboriginal people being in the Army was a positive experience because, for the first time, they were treated as allies and almost as equals.

Three

Controlling the Natives

. . . controlling the drift of natives from Arnhem Land Reserve to town and military centres along the North–South road and for preventing contact of natives with miners and Australian Works Council camps in the Maranboy district.

Report on the Administration of the Northern Territory for the year 1945–46, on the purpose of establishing the Maranboy Native Settlement

After the War

The Second World War accelerated contact between Aboriginals and non-Aboriginals in the Northern Territory. After their wartime experiences, Aboriginals throughout the Arnhem Land Reserve increasingly sought contact with the European economy. As Berndt and Berndt[1] note, the heightened activity associated with Army-camp life altered the tempo of Indigenous life and disturbed patterns in traditional ceremonies and food-collecting to a far greater degree than had hitherto been experienced. The Katherine township found itself in a difficult position after the war, since the availability of Aboriginal labour and its increased purchasing power had become important to the town economy but the physical presence of Aboriginal people, particularly those from remote communities, was not acceptable to the townspeople.[2] During the post-war period the immediate area around townships such as Katherine continued to be prohibited to Aboriginals. Often, these prohibited areas were extended in order to incorporate the growth of the town that had occurred during the war. As Lea[3] states 'Aborigines were welcome, their dollars were welcome, as long as they behaved themselves and settled in the periphery far removed from strategic areas where their presence constituted an embarrassment and lowered land values'.

During this period there was a major movement of Aboriginal people away from reserves towards Darwin and other major population centres. Controlling this drift became a cornerstone of Native Affairs Branch policy, and the establishment of 'native settlements' became a major strategy to implement this policy. The Maranboy Native Settlement, established in 1943, was the first of these settlements in the Barunga–Wugularr region. Its stated purpose was to control the drift of Aboriginal people from the Arnhem Land reserve. This settlement also served as a dispersal depot when Aboriginal people were discharged from Army Control Camps at Larrimah, Mataranka and Katherine. The number of Aboriginal people living there on June 30th 1946 was 420. In January 1949, Patrol Officer Kyle-Little articulated this problem in a report to the Native Affairs Branch:

> The war has brought about big changes in the native economic life and has tended to accelerate contact with our culture. Natives throughout the Arnhem Land Reserve – many of whom worked with the Services during the war – now desire to participate in our economic and social life, and unless the latter activities are advanced and some attractions made in the Reserve, the Native Affairs Branch will be unable to cope with the already ever-increasing drift of natives from this Reserve to Darwin and other settlements along the North-South highway.[4]

Joe's Garden

The settlement that became known as Joe's Garden was established late in 1943 in response to adverse comments by the European community about 'native control' at Maranboy. It was a Native Affairs Branch Control Depot, situated approximately 12 kilometres (7.5 miles) from the Maranboy mines on land owned by Joseph Israelson, who was appointed Superintendent on a salary of £4 10s. per week. With the help of Aboriginal people, Israelson developed an extensive vegetable garden for military and Aboriginal use.

Joe's Garden, located on Jawoyn land known as Guymanluk, was an important ceremonial site prior to the area coming under European control.[5] What is possibly the last recorded instance of the use of this site for ceremonial purposes was in 1948, when around 100 Aboriginal people from Katherine, Maranboy and Mataranka are said to have spent an extended period there in order to participate in a ceremony. The settlement at Joe's Garden was intended to hold Aboriginal people from a range of language groups and it is clear from the documents of the period that these language groups

Figure 3.1
Aboriginal people with Joe Israelson, c. 1940s
Northern Territory Library, PH0510/1377 Harney/McCaffery Collection

had been living in the area for some time. For example, a 1945 report by V.J. White stated that the 'Jauan, Youngman and Miellie' language groups had coexisted harmoniously at Maranboy for many years and that 'it could be said that the Maranboy district is the country of their adoption, and that they are permanent residents of the Area'.[6] The numbers of Aboriginal people from different language groups who lived at Katherine, Maranboy and Mataranka during 1942, clearly reflects this co-existence.

The first Aboriginal workers at Joe's Garden were paid only in rations, clothing and tobacco, though at that time, such working conditions were usual in the Territory. For example, Aboriginal guides assisting Native Affairs Branch Patrol Officers in Arnhem

Language Group	Men	Women	Children	Total
Djauan (Jawoyn)	74	40	9	123
Maiali (Mielli)	55	35	25	115
Ngalkbun (Ngalkpon)	49	43	33	125
Rembarrnga	42	34	24	100
Yangman	22	16	5	43

Table 3.1
Census of Aboriginal language groups at Katherine, Maranboy and Mataranka in 1942

Land were paid only one third of a stick of tobacco per day and, as noted previously, tobacco, clothing and rations were the only standard pay on the Maranboy tinfield.[7] Older Aboriginal people do not today recall any major issues of clothing at either Joe's Garden or the Maranboy fields.

The settlement at Joe's Garden developed extensive vegetable gardens. Magnolia Rankin had fond memories of this place:

> Joe Garden . . . long time ago, might be that garden him work out [is finished] now. Him all right before, lot of tucker . . . tomato, pumpkin, cabbage, watermelon, banana. They bin grow em up now, longa Joe Garden. Potato, too. Onion, him grow up too. Him bin good man.[8]

At times it was difficult to augment the garden produce with enough meat for local Aboriginal people and a comprehensive correspondence exists concerning a request for authority to purchase beef. These requests were refused by the Government Secretary on the grounds that 'natives cannot be fed in idleness if the funds are not available' and it was suggested that Aboriginal people might be sent bush to forage for themselves. V.G. Carrington, the Acting Director of Native Affairs, expressed his assessment of the situation:

> The natives, unfortunately, will not be content to starve or go without meat while funds are being obtained and no doubt many will disperse to townships, railway camps, etc., where we may expect a revival of methylated spirits drinking, prostitution and other vices with their attendant results . . . I suggest that as there will probably be a good deal of criticism, the Administrator should be informed of the position.[9]

King River Compound

In 1946 around 420 Aboriginal people were settled at the King River Compound, approximately 10 kilometres from Joe's Garden. The Jawoyn name for this site is *Durrk-gamernggarlan*.[10] The King River Compound absorbed Aboriginal people from a range of Army Control Camps and also from Native Affairs Branch Control Depots near Maranboy and Katherine. The existing control depot at Joe's Garden was considered to be too close to the Maranboy mines, while that at Katherine was thought to be too close to the township – and both were considered to be too close to the North–South road. One of the main objectives was to minimise 'undesirable contact' between, mainly, European men and Aboriginal women.

That the issue was one of control is clearly shown in the statement by V.J. White when he put forward his proposal for the establishment of the King River Compound:

> The establishment of a settlement would enable complete control of natives along the [north–south] railway line, and any disregard of instruction issued to them to remain at Maranboy Settlement, or to return to their Reserve, could be met by removal to Melville Island.
>
> I consider that if vigorous patrols were undertaken by Patrol Officers, that these, together with police co-operation at Pine Creek, Katherine and Mataranka, would purge these centres of the undesirable element of the past.[11]

The King River Compound was well-watered but the soil was poor and it soon became obvious that it was not going to be tenable as a long-term proposition. In 1947, only 18 months after its establishment, it was abandoned in favour of a new location at Tandangal, near Beswick station.

Tandangal

The Tandangal Native Settlement, from the Jawoyn *dangdangdal*, was established in 1947 but lasted only until 1951. Also known as the Eight Mile Settlement since it was located about 13 kilometres (8 miles) from the Beswick station homestead, it was intended to hold a number of language groups including the Jawoyn, Ngalkpon, Rembarrnga, Mielli and Yargaman. Its establishment, operation and failure highlights the interplay of power relations between white administrators and local Aboriginal people. In a sense the settlement was doomed from the start, since its location was selected without obtaining advice from local Aboriginals, the people best qualified to assess its viability.

This error was compounded by the manner in which the resettlement of Aboriginal people from the King River Compound to Tandangal was effected. District Superintendent G. Sweeney described this resettlement in a memorandum to the Acting Director of Native Affairs:

> The move was made at the end of October, the hottest time of the year. Transport was provided for only three aged sick natives, the remainder

> were told to walk the twenty-eight miles from King River to the new Settlement. The manager of Beswick Station refused to supply transport for the movement of the natives. There was little water on the road and many of the native women had young children, and a number had infants in arms.[12]

Victor Hood recalled this trip:

> After him finished, we got to go Tandangal. No motor car. They walking. They carrying their swag. No more have water, they had shipped this other place, war camp. That welfare man, he had a motor car. One fella whiteman who would always walk and smoke the smoke. He looked at the sick people and took them to hospital. He used to give that smoke, not this tin one, block one, you got to cut him with a knife. Mr Ryan [Patrol Officer Ryan], he was a big boss, he lived in Katherine. He's died now, too old.
>
> They bin walk there, Tandangal. That same olgaman [Phyllis Wiynjorroc's mother] him cooked the tucker. Everybody used to cook him. Damper, johnny cake and beef. Ring the bell for lunch and maybe tea, so people can come. Billy can each, for tea. They had the biggest copper full of tea. They used to have a little cup, fill up one billy can, another billy can. They used to line them up. Not just one person was cooking. One boss [Phyllis' mother]. That tucker went to all the different families.
>
> And that old Gela [Phyllis' father, Charlie Lamjerroc], he used to have two wives. One Barawuli (Bulainjan). Another olgaman bin Bulainjan, again, bla Anderson mob.[13]

The choice of location and the method of their removal was objected to by Aboriginal people. Phyllis Wiynjorroc's father, Charlie Lamjerroc, the senior traditional owner for the area at that time, actively opposed the choice of site and encouraged others to resist through a policy of non-co-operation. Lamjerroc was very vocal in his objections, as by Aboriginal lore he held overall responsibility for the general welfare of his community. Peter Manabaru attributed the problems with the site to a lack of space and water:

> Only a little bit spring water, not enough water. Not a big spring, like Barunga. Him got no spring water, only mud. They didn't want to drink that. No rainfall, [except] every raintime him get a little bit water. Him no good. Ola kid bin sick. No enough houses, area to put a

> house. At Barunga you can bogie [wash] everywhere. Not enough water at Tandangal, that's why people been shift longa Bamyili.[14]

In the end, Lamjerroc was banished from Tandangal by Fraser-Allen, the Superintendent of the settlement, for indiscipline.

> The headman of the Tandangal area, Charlie Lamburag (Djauan), had to be banished for indiscipline. He would have been a power of help if his co-operation had been won.[15]

However, Lamjerroc's removal did more than dispel a proven 'trouble-maker' – it also placed the leader of the people outside the settlement, weakening any cohesive sense of identity that might have been developing within the community.

There were two main reasons behind this strong Aboriginal resistance to settlement at Tangandal. The first is that people felt that the area was very powerful and dangerous, not least because a cave near Tandangal was used as the final resting place of human bones. The second reason was that Aboriginal people were aware of the water-quality problems that existed at the site: the basic supply came from a small spring that, in the end, proved to be totally inadequate. On two counts, then, there existed a fear that Tandangal was not a healthy place to live. Soon after the settlement was occupied there were three deaths, possibly exacerbated by the rigours of removal – an old woman, and two sisters who were described in reports as being in the prime of life. Aboriginal people attributed the deaths of these women to polluted water. According to District Superintendent Sweeney, these deaths confirmed the fears that Aboriginal people already held concerning this location.[16] This problem intensified when the opening up of water holes interfered with the Dreaming associations of the area.

Consequently, only 60 of the 200 people who had left the King River Compound chose to move to Tandangal Native Settlement.[17] The remainder scattered in small groups around the Maranboy, Beswick and Waterhouse areas, living off 'bush tucker' such as goannas, shellfish, wild honey and lily roots. The resistance was ongoing and on 25th February 1948, Patrol Officer Sweeney reported:

> We located a camp of natives on a permanent waterhole. There were four aged natives, including one blind man, two able bodied natives

> and three children in the camp. They had formerly been at Joe Israelson's and the King Compound. We asked them why they had not come into Tangandal. They replied 'We would rather die where we are than in that place'. We asked them what their objection was. They replied, 'Too many people have died there already'.
>
> They refused to come into the Settlement. We talked to them for some time and later they said they would come into the Settlement later. But we felt they were not convinced and were only giving us the 'Pleasing answer'.[18]

The 'pleasing answer' is that which Aboriginal people give when non-Aboriginal people insist upon them acting against their own wishes.

The refusal of so many Aboriginal people to move to Tandangal created a situation in which most Aboriginal people in the region were living outside the control of government administrated centres, constituting a threat not only to the authority and prestige of the manager of Beswick station, Mr Syms, but also to the overall system of containment and control. Syms wrote that he could not 'allow wandering natives to roam about his cattle feeding areas or camp on the waterholes used by the cattle'. One solution that he raised was tantamount to the establishment of a concentration camp: he suggested fencing off several square kilometres around Tandangal and stationing a patrol officer at Beswick station in order to forcibly return Aboriginal people to the settlement. Fortunately for Aboriginal and non-Aboriginal relations at that time, this solution was not implemented.

The Aboriginal people who worked at the Tandangal settlement were paid 10s. a week. Patrol Officer Evans commented that these people were working 'very hard' and recommended that the wages of the 'more energetic and willing' workers be increased to £1 per week. These wages need to be considered in terms of what the money could buy at that time. In 1949 the Tandangal canteen was selling the following items: print material at 3s. 9d. per yard, cotton frocks at 21s. each, smoking pipes at 3s. 6d. each, hanging mirrors at 1s. 9d., soap at 6d. per cake, handkerchiefs at 1s. 4d. each, khaki riding trousers at 16s., 'Gem' razor blades at 2s. the packet and leather waist belts at 3s. 3d. each.[19] The wages of Aboriginal peoples at Tandangal were paid into the Aboriginal Trust Fund and, once again, were not readily accessible to the people who earned them: they could only be drawn with the approval of the Superintendant.

The history of the settlement at Tandangal highlights the arrogance of white administrators and the relative powerlessness of local Aboriginal people. Even the decision to abandon the settlement was made on the advice of administrators, not of the people who were expected to live there. Tandangal was an unsuitable choice for many reasons, among them a religious restrictions on living in the area and a lack of sufficient permanent water to sustain a settlement. A series of poor decisions by white administrators resulted in extremely primitive living conditions for Aboriginal people, conditions that did not improve during the entire time the settlement was occupied. The only substantial buildings were the communal kitchen and bathroom and the accommodation for non-Aboriginal staff, while Aboriginal people lived in humpies they built for themselves. In 1950 Patrol Officer Evans reported that the stoves in the native kitchen were 'useless' and that the condition of the clothing of Aboriginal people was 'very poor'. Two months before the settlement was finally abandoned, Senior Education Officer Newby reported that there were no toilets for Aboriginal use and only one shower. Moreover, there was never sufficient water for bathing and Aboriginal people often complained of this to visiting officials. At one stage the springs dried up entirely and even drinking water had to be carted in. At last, Tandangal was condemned and in June 1951 Aboriginal people moved to a new site, initially known as Beswick Creek Native Settlement.

Four

Stockman Time

They used to work mustering cattle to quieten them you know. People used to do it, and they would give them a little stick of tobacco, a little bit of tucker. They learnt to ride well. They gave them tucker to make them quiet. Then they were really quiet, those people. They got to know them.

Georgie Jaurdaku[1]

Beswick Station

An integral part of the Australian Aboriginal history is that period when people worked on cattle stations. Senior Aboriginal people today refer to this period as 'stockman time'.[2] The first claimants for pastoral land in the Barunga–Wugularr region included Mick Madrill, who had previously been a packhorse mailman and a miner at Maranboy. In 1920 he was issued with a pastoral lease over 154 square miles (399 sq. km) that lay to the west of the 100 square miles (259 sq. km) claimed by his friend Jack Shuter, the shopkeeper at Maranboy.[3] The land claimed by Madrill became known as Beswick station.

These were rough times. Like other pastoralists of the time, Madrill soon developed the reputation of being a hard man. Daisy Borduk remembered that Madrill became angry when Aboriginal people disturbed the cattle around his waterholes and she said that he used to shoot at people to frighten them away from his cattle and 'sometimes he meant it, too'.[4] In those days, reporting Madrill's actions to the police was not an option. In fact, Madrill's complaints about his cattle being disturbed by Aboriginal people were supported by local police, who almost certainly endorsed his methods for maintaining control. Constable Vic Hall's view was:

> The unrestricted presence of Aboriginals on a pastoral lease is entirely disastrous to the purpose of the pioneer cattleman.[5]

Madrill was a problem for Aboriginal women, too. On one occasion Daisy Borduk's sister protected herself from him by threatening to hit him with a large stick. Madrill's reputation for violence is recorded by Forrest,[6] who states that Madrill and Jack Shuter were both responsible for shooting Aboriginal people.[7]

Eventually, Madrill's relationship with local Aboriginal people turned into outright conflict. Daisy Borduk[8] recalled that after a particularly provoking incident the Aboriginal elders decided to kill Madrill 'ceremony way'. They put his faeces in a hole in a bloodwood tree and sealed it with sugar bag (wild honey) wax after they had sung it to make sure he would die. A while later Madrill got very sick and called out for people to help him. 'Help me, somebody help me'. No-one came and finally, he was sent to hospital in Adelaide where he died. That bloodwood tree still stands. Peter Manabaru recalls:

> Mick Madrill, he hated the old people. In the old days people had a dog, he had a lot of cattle, that's why he didn't like them. Mike Madrill, him say: 'We don't want this fucking myall blackfella around this area'. Then him shoot around, try and shoot the people. Cheeky bastard, too, that head stockman for him. They bin kill him, that Mick Madrill. One clever man, old man. One of the stockmen, old Dick, bin kill him, him own boss, because him bin cruel all day to the old people. Blackfella rule, they bin base that ironwood tree, they put in everything longa there, then close him up, and put wax [over that hole] and then him bin finish.[9]

A few months before Madrill died in May 1942 he made E.J. Collins a partner in Beswick station.[10] After Madrill's death the property became jointly owned by Edward Collins, known locally as 'Cowboy Collins', and Mrs Connie Madrill, the widow of Mick Madrill. These two continued to add to their holdings until Beswick station consisted of three pastoral leases including Jack Shuter's original claim. In total, the original 154 square miles was increased to 581 square miles.

Ted Collins and his wife Anna moved into Madrill's house during 1942 but began building a substantial new homestead soon after. The new house had three bedrooms, an office, a large living room, a dining room and a lounge area, with a walkway to a separate kitchen and bathroom. Outbuildings constructed of corrugated iron included a storeroom, butcher shop and kitchen for Aboriginal people.[11] Aboriginal women such as Daisy Borduk helped with the housework and cooking for the stockmen, but Anna Collins always cooked for herself and Ted.

Figure 4.1
Gooburrumban, his wife, Peggy Woodroff, and their baby, Brian, c. 1949
UQFL18/2020, Erenestine Hill collection, Fryer collection, University of Queensland

Cowboy Collins continued Madrill's rough ways of living. David Blanarsi recalled that Cowboy Collins used to shoot Aboriginal people's billy cans to stop them having a cup of tea when he felt they should have been working.[12]

In April, 1947 Beswick station was bought by the Native Affairs Branch in order to establish a Government Training Station for Natives. Delivered with 2,000 head of cattle and around 100 horses, it fetched £6,734.[13] The purpose of the training station was to supply meat for native settlements, produce a surplus of stock for sale and to train Aboriginals as stockmen.[14] To this end, the existing 581 square miles was augmented with 250 square miles of vacant Crown land to the north and 142 square miles to the south. Beswick station now totalled 973 square miles in all[15] and formed a real presence in the region.

This was a period in which day-to-day life was hard for Aboriginal people but it was life with a purpose. Women as well as men worked the stock. Alma Gibbs describes conditions at Mainoru station from a woman's point of view:

> When Jimmy Gibbs and I came back to Mainoru, horses were everywhere. I was a stock girl then. I liked it. I used to ride horses, tailing

bullocks. Get up at maybe 4 o'clock, make tea, 5 o'clock have breakfast, 6 o'clock we'd go. Like that.

They were really hard-work times then. We've got easy one now. We can get up when we like. Before it was no good. Rough one. We used to work, no money, no wages. Only ration – blanket, boot, hat, tobacco, free. We worked for rations.[16]

Figure 4.2
Tex Camfoo breaking in a brumby at Mainoru station
MAGNT, Pict 047, Dodd Collection

The establishment of Beswick Government Training Station for Natives articulated with the plans of the Northern Territory government to expand the pastoral industry. The training and supply of Aboriginal labour to stations in the Territory was an essential part of that strategy. The report on the Administration of the Northern Territory for Year 1943–44 stated that:

> I am convinced that the future of the Northern Territory is bound up in the development and prosperity of the pastoral industry. This development and prosperity can only be attainment by the pastoral areas of the Territory being put to their proper and full uses.

As with the mining industry, access to Aboriginal labour and expertise was critical to achieving this prosperity, something of which Europeans were consciously aware. The report on the

Figure 4.3
Chuckaduck Lindsay, Head Stockman, Mainaru station
MAGNT, Pict 047, Dodd Collection

Administration of the Northern Territory for Year 1944–45 reinforces the view of Nelson Johnson, the former United States Ambassador to Australia, that:

> Without the Australian aboriginal these great cattle stations could not function at present, for the aboriginal ('abo' as more familiarly known) is the stockrider of the country, who assists the stockmen in rounding up, or 'mustering' the herds that are to be branded, inoculated and sent to market. With an unerring knowledge of the country and an uncanny ability to follow the trail of anything that moves, he can find wandering stock or horses and survive in a waterless, foodless area where the white men would perish.

Patrol Officer Ryan's report in January, 1950 discussed this issue:

> I have often thought that Beswick station would be a good place for a school for male half-caste children. The removal of half-caste boys from cattle stations to missions for education brings about the loss of valuable labour to the pastoral industry and means that the half-caste children lack training in a pursuit for which they are naturally adapted.[17]

Forms of Control

Like other settlements established in the Barunga–Wugularr region, controlling the natives was the main purpose of the Beswick Creek Native Settlement. At this stage in the social history of the region, the main forms of control that were used were restricting the physical movements of Aboriginal people, including the use of the settlement as a de facto prison farm; denying Aboriginal people access to money and the freedom to spend it in whichever way they chose; and through racially based legislation that restricted their normal human rights, such as the right to bring up their children or to own the same number of dogs as Europeans. The matter of the removal of children of mixed descent from Aboriginal mothers is perhaps the cruelest of the devices used to break the spirit of Aboriginal people in this and other regions and is dealt with in Chapter Seven.

One of the major ways in which European administrators controlled Aboriginal behaviour and undermined Indigenous culture was by the removal of 'troublemakers' from their home communities to Native Settlements. Beswick Creek was one of a series of such settlements that were used as prison farms and to which people were committed for extended periods depending on their 'crimes' – and even misdemeanors could incur great penalties. For instance, in June 1952 Dick Lim of Darwin was committed to Beswick Creek Native Settlement for 12 months for 'drinking liquor'; in March, 1955, Nandua of Groote Eylandt was sentenced to 12 months for 'fighting' while Paul Ulgarking was sentenced to 6 months for 'using indecent language'. Ulgarking's sentencing was reported to the Welfare Branch by Patrol Officer Penhall:

> Aboriginal Paul Ulgarking from Roper Mission was charged with using indecent language, the facts of this case being that Rev. Leske of Roper Mission had approached Paul and asked him to commence work. Paul did not appear to be enthusiastic. When Rev. Leske insisted that he start work, Paul became cheeky and answered 'all right, all right, leave me alone, you *** mongrel'. Rev. Leske reported the matter to Constable Haag, and Paul was arrested on the present charge. He was sentenced to the rising of the Court, with a recommendation that he be committed to the Beswick Creek Native Settlement for a period of six months.[18]

Another important way in which people were controlled was through denying them the power that comes with having money to spend. When Beswick Creek Native Settlement was first established there was some hope of a degree of fiscal autonomy for Aboriginal people, since for a short time they were paid in cash. However, there were huge discrepancies between the wages paid to Aboriginal and non-Aboriginal people. The initial wage paid to Aboriginals at Beswick was 5s. per week for both women and men working in positions such as gardeners, kitchen maids and goat shepherds; 15s. per week for stockmen and horse-tailers, and 10s. a week for men employed on a casual basis.[19] For many years, housing was not provided for Aboriginal people, other than the humpies they built themselves. However, by 17th July 1947, the wages had been adjusted so that women in jobs such as goat shepherd and general domestic help were paid 5s. per week, while men who worked as gardeners or yardmen were paid 10s. per week. Stockmen's wages ranged from 12s. 6d. per week in their first year to £1 per week in their fourth and subsequent years. Nevertheless, the Pastoral Award for (overwhelmingly white) cooks catering for from 13 to 30 people was at this time £4 2s. per week and at Beswick Station in October 1947 a cook was employed at the award rate.[20] Aboriginals were 'included as persons for this purpose', though the manager at Beswick counted 'two aboriginals as one person'.

However, the level of fiscal autonomy enjoyed by Aboriginal people at Beswick was short-lived and on 1st July 1947, F.H. Moy, the Director of the Native Affairs Branch, instructed the accountant that the full wages of native staff at the station had to be paid into the Aboriginals' Trust Account.[21] Since it was virtually impossible for Aboriginal people to obtain this money, this meant that they effectively were only paid for their labour in kind. Native Affairs advised the station of the appropriate accounting procedure:

> It is standard practice on stations to sell native employees rations, clothing and trade goods which they are unable to purchase elsewhere owing to the remoteness of the station from shopping centres. In consequence the Manager of the [Beswick] station will be permitted to sell these items to native employees. He will be required to keep a record of all such debits against an employee's account.[22]

This period at Beswick was a transitional one for Aboriginal people. Many were still living a bush lifestyle but those who decided to live on the stations increasingly came to adopt the outward manifestations of European culture, such as clothing and other material goods. The coexistence of these two ways of living can be seen in the clothing worn by Aboriginal people in Figures 4.1 and 4.4.

Figure 4.4
Aboriginal people at Beswick, 1949. Daisy Borduk possibly on the right. (Joyce Fuller Collection, Northern Territory Archives, Darwin).

It would be a mistake, however, to construe the use and adaptation of European clothing and/or material culture as a breakdown in the social order of Aboriginal people. It is much more difficult to identify changes in social structures and cultural values – and variations in such things do not necessarily coincide with changes in material culture.

The manager of Beswick station was responsible for the health of the Aboriginal people who lived there. This excerpt from the manager's report records an extraordinary number of people visiting the nurse, Mrs Fuller, during 1953:

> Medical supervision is in charge of Mrs J. Fuller who is fully qualified and a currently registered nurse with the Department of Health. For the year there were 4,331 attendances – a number that exceeds many hospitals.
>
> To Mrs Fuller goes the credit that no deaths occurred at this Station. This is due to her correct diagnosis and proper treatment. A perusal of her medical records will confirm this.
>
> Medical parades are held both morning and evening and Mrs Fuller is on call at any time in an emergency or when any patient requires

> special treatment. The natives are trained to report any sickness and to come for treatment . . . It is to be recorded that Mrs Fuller has not received any remuneration for her valuable work since she commenced in December, 1952.[23]

Not all of these visits would have been motivated by ill health. Some would have been ethnographic forays by Aboriginal people, intent on familiarising themselves with European practices. A related European eccentricity would have been the 'medical parades' that Mrs Fuller held in the morning and evening. While this may suggest that some aspects of Aboriginal people's lives were subject to some regimentation, it quite possible that those on parade did not take this seriously.

Dogs Matter

Some of the most oppressive ways in which Indigenous people were controlled, however, was through legislatively endorsed and racially based restrictions on their normal human rights. For example, one of the ordinances which Aboriginal people found most odious were those restricting their right to own dogs. This was an example of the gulf in understanding between whites and Aboriginals, demonstrating both white people's fundamental misunderstanding of Aboriginal society and their lack of sympathy with long-established cultural practices. Dogs had been an invaluable adjunct to Aboriginal hunting strategies since the dingo had been brought from south-east Asia around 4,000 years before and, if anything, had become even more valuable to hunting in the colonial period, when Aboriginals were prevented from owning guns without a special licence.

European control over this aspect of Indigenous affairs has a legislative history spanning more than sixty years. It was instigated with the Dog Ordinance of 1923, which stated that any 'unregistered dogs in excess of one, kept by any Aboriginal outside the limits of any Municipal Area, may be destroyed by any police officer, protector of Aboriginals, or person thereto authorised by the Administrator'. This ordinance was refined into the Registration of Dogs Ordinance, 1938, that stated that 'if any aboriginal native is found keeping more than one unregistered dog, any Registrar, Protector of Aboriginals or person thereto authorised in writing by the Administrator may kill all such unregistered in excess of one'.

There are many injustices involved here, one of which is that even though they worked, Aboriginal people were not paid in cash which could be used to pay for dog registration. The statutory recognition that Aboriginal people may not be able to pay these fees did not come until the Registration of Dogs Ordinance, 1955, which allowed Aboriginals to register a dog without any fee if they were unable to obtain employment 'by reason of age, infirmity, or mode of living'. Aboriginal people lived under the burden of various dog ordinances for a large part of the twentieth century since they were not repealed until the enactment of the Registration of Dogs Ordinance 1964.

The traditional wisdom assuaging any European guilt over these matters is that the ordinances were aimed at reducing Aboriginal health problems associated with their close relationships to dogs. At a practical level, they pre-empted European criticism of the Native Affairs Branch over the number of dogs in native settlements. Accordingly, at least once a year during the 1940s and 1950s, all personnel on these settlements were directed to destroy all dogs pursuant to the 1938 ordinance. As the Acting Director of Native Affairs, R.K. McCaffery, noted in correspondence to the Government Secretary during 1953, this placed 'the staff on Settlements in an unfortunate, invidious position with the natives, as more often than not the favourite dog of the native is shot and bitterness ensues'. The total inability of European administrators to understand the Aboriginal position is demonstrated in McCaffery's solution, enacted in the 1955 ordinance, which was to legislate to 'permit an aboriginal (ward) one registration without fee'. He expressed his confidence 'that this procedure would remove the only real objection that natives could sustain when their dogs are destroyed'. This comment displays massive ignorance of Aboriginal feelings on this matter.

Aboriginal people are very astute politically and were well aware that this law was about controlling them specifically as a group. This is evident in the following account by Alma Gibbs of an incident which occurred at Mountain Valley:

> Another manager came. Johnny Doyle. Then Johnny shot my dog. He was going to shoot him but I said 'You can't shoot my dog. You've got dogs, too.'
>
> He said 'I'll have to shoot one of them'.

> I said 'Alright. If you shoot my dog, I'm going. I've got to leave here. I'm not going to work for you now. Finish.' And I kept going then. When teacher went on their holiday they gave me a lift to Beswick. I took the two dogs. Johnny Doyle wanted to bring me back. No, I give him no chance more. I don't know why he wanted to shoot my dog. He had dogs, too. If I'd had a gun I'd have shot his dog too.[24]

But there was little that Aboriginal people could do. The issue here isn't just that of killing dogs in order to make people's homes more hygienic, the reasoning accepted by non-Aboriginal people. Dogs have been an important part of Indigenous Australian social structures for at least 4,000 years, so the attacks on the dogs were incursions on traditional social structures, as well as on the autonomy of the their owners. Because they were used for hunting, dogs were economically important to the Aboriginals. This was especially important given the *Firearms Ordinance*, which prohibited Aboriginal people from owning guns without a special license. Moreover, as Alma Gibbs clearly understood, this legislation was racially discriminatory.

The problem was not only in the legislation itself, but also in the arbitrary manner in which it could be implemented. In September 1952 Constable J.A. Cooke reported that 'Mr McKay told me the blacks have a tremendous number of dogs but myself I only saw a few and managed to shoot only twenty-five'. Daisy Borduk describes the actions of Mick Madrill, the original owner of Beswick station:

> He saw those pup-pups [puppies] owned by that old woman: 'Ah, You got too many ... I'm going to take those pup-pups for you' ... He took them near that big billabong there ... and killed them with a stick and busted them on a rock. Then he got them in a bag and took them to that old woman ... She cried for those dogs when she saw all the dead ones and blood ... everywhere. Grandma for that Peter Manabaru, she went bush then ... to that cave, Bambaluk.[25]

Given the fondness that Barunga people have for their dogs, the manner in which their animals were treated by Europeans during this period is a real indicator of how disempowered Aboriginal people felt at the time, but no matter what their personal feelings, they couldn't stop Europeans from killing their dogs. All they could do was leave those places and those people.

Five

Government Time

The Settlement will serve as a medical, educational and training centre for the natives, and will hold any drift of natives from the Arnhem Land Reserve coming down through Mainoru. The Settlement will also serve as a home for the old people and for dependants of able bodied natives who leave the Settlement for employment outside. The Settlement provides stock boys and other labour for Beswick Station and stock boys for droving and surrounding Stations as required

District Superintendent Sweeney, on the purpose of Bamyili settlement[1]

Aboriginal people in northern Australia use the phrase 'government time' to refer to the assimilation era, that period during which their daily lives were under the direct control of government officials. This era commenced at the end of the second world war, when it became feasible to implement the assimilation policies mooted at the 1937 conference of Commonwealth and State Aboriginal Authorities, and continued through to the 1970s. Government policy during this period was based on the premise that Aboriginal people would eventually adopt a lifestyle similar to that of Europeans.

Assimilation Policy

The implementation of assimilation policy in the Northern Territory had two clear phases. The first extended protectionist policy and was primarily concerned with encouraging people of mixed descent to take up a European way of life and with the continued segregation of people of entirely Aboriginal descent. The second, more insidious, phase was developed during the 1950s and was explicitly concerned with the 'social, economic and political advancement' of Aboriginal people. This policy was especially damaging since it aimed to transform Aboriginal society by replacing their cultural knowledge with European values and controlling their movement across their lands.

The primary legislation used to implement assimilation policy during the 1950s and 1960s was the *Welfare Ordinance* of 1953, promoted by the Minister for the Territories, Paul Hasluck. Its genesis was in the Native Welfare Conference of 1951, which Hasluck was instrumental in convening. The stated aim of the ordinance was to promote the 'social, economic and political advancement' of wards 'for the purpose of assisting them and their descendants to take their place as members of the community of the Commonwealth'. Though it was flawed in many respects, the legislation was thought to be an advance in policies dealing with Aboriginal people. Lovegrove[2] comments that it represented a major change in the attitudes of Europeans to Aboriginals, in that it dealt with care and assistance to 'certain persons' rather than to a particular race of people. However, the wording was still aimed at Aboriginal people, demonstrated in part by its enactment coinciding with the repealing of the *Aboriginals Ordinance* 1918–53, and it was still paternal, prohibiting and protective. Cowlishaw refers to this ordinance as 'Hasluck's final solution', describing it as:

> . . . a legislative move of brilliant simplicity . . . which eradicated 'Aborigines' from the legislation, replacing them with 'wards' by a definitional sleight of hand. The Aboriginals Ordinance would become the Welfare Ordinance, no longer applying to a race, but to those who were unable to look after themselves.[3]

During this period Hasluck used assimilation policies to actively pursue what he judged to be the interests of Aboriginal people. His speech in the Estimates Debate in the House of Representatives on the 6th October 1955 attempted to identify the conditions under which Aboriginal people might be assimilated into European society:

> . . . we have to give attention to their *health*. So long as there are native people subject to leprosy, or any other so-called loathsome disease, so long will there be exclusion. We have to give attention to *hygiene*. So long as natives are not living in a way that makes them physically acceptable – to put it crudely, so long as natives live in a way that makes them smell – then there is no hope for them. We have to improve their hygiene in order to make them acceptable. We have to give them *education*. Unless they can speak English well, and also express their thoughts fairly well, there will be no acceptance. We have to give them *jobs*. Unless they can earn their living, unless they can sustain the sort of life to which we are attempting to raise them,

> the attempt to raise them to that higher life will be in vain . . . And over and above that . . . is to make sure that those who have reached that desirable level also can get *housing* (emphases added).[4]

This statement not only identifies Hasluck's priority areas of health, hygiene, education, jobs and housing but also makes it clear that in his view the major barrier to the successful implementation of assimilation policies was acceptance of Aboriginal people by the wider European community. The support of this community was sought in educational publications produced by the federal government. One series of booklets was particularly widely distributed and included *Assimilation of Our Aborigines*,[5] *Skills of Our Aborigines*,[6] *One People*,[7] *Our Aborigines*[8] and *Fringe Dwellers*.[9] In *Our Aborigines*, assimilation was presented to the Australian public in the following terms:

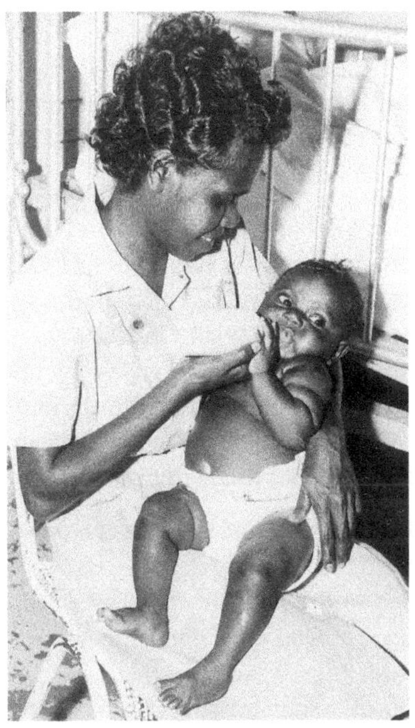

Figure 5.1
Janet Turner and baby
AIP5, MAGNT, PIC 047,
Dodd Collection

> . . . the policy of assimilation means in the view of all Australian governments that all aborigines and part-aborigines are expected eventually to attain the same manner of living as other Australians and to live as members of a single Australian community enjoying the same rights and privileges, accepting the same responsibilities, observing the same customs and influenced by the same beliefs, hopes and loyalties as other Australians.[10]

From an assimilation viewpoint, the only successful Aboriginals were those who took on European values. This was symbolised graphically in the many photographs of smartly dressed Aboriginals being taught tasks appropriate to a European lifestyle by teachers who were of either European or mixed descent. These values are implicit in Figure 5.1, which shows Janet Turner, dressed in a nurse's uniform and bottle feeding a baby at Mainoru station.

Bamyili: A Medical, Educational and Training Centre for Natives

The Beswick Creek Native Settlement was established as part of the Beswick station training scheme. The site of this settlement was chosen in 1951, when it became apparent that there was an urgent need to abandon the Tandangal settlement and after several attempts to locate additional water supplies at Charaluk, the original choice for the settlement adjacent to Beswick, had failed. Victor Hood described the move from Tandangal.

> They sit down there [at Tandangal]. Not enough water, again, and not much room. Hill this side, hill that side. Too many people for that place. And they were thinking 'How can we go from that place?' They were thinking about another place. They were walking. Not too many motor car, just carrying that tucker, petrol. The people carried their swags themselves. All the kids, too, they were carrying things on their shoulders. Biggest load. Long walk, la Bamyili.[11]

The location that was finally selected had been the site of the Beswick homestead up until 1944 and was 40 kilometres closer than Beswick station to the Maranboy mines and the main highway. It was on high, well-drained country with Beswick Creek providing permanent water and was joined to the Stuart highway by an all-weather road which gave access to the settlement throughout the year. A report by the Native Welfare Branch of the Northern Territory[12] states that the express purpose of this settlement was:

- To bring natives together in a community and to teach them the habits and skills of living in such a community.
- To provide welfare services fitted to the needs of the people concerned bearing in mind the stage of social development they have attained.
- To provide a means whereby education and training may be given, particularly to children and adults.
- To introduce the general concept of 'work' as a worthwhile aim in life.
- To develop in the younger and middle-aged groups an attitude that settlements (and mission stations) are there to provide health and

educational facilities for children, so that the latter may be prepared for a future life as adults living in a wider community than the tribe.

- To provide a temporary home wherever necessary for natives in transit.

The implementation of assimilation policies during the 1950s and 1960s produced a substantive infrastructure at the Beswick Creek Native Settlement, which in 1953 was fully operational. Produce gardens had been established and a range of buildings erected, including storehouses, visitors quarters, a native kitchen and dining room and a pump house. Aboriginal housing was in the form of Econo Huts, the dimensions of which were 15 x 10 feet (approximately 4.5 x 3 metres) with a cantilevered verandah 6 feet wide (see example in Figure 5.2). These were built in groups of eight, and gender-segregated showers and pit toilets were provided for each group.[13] During this period 200 Aboriginal people were normally resident at the settlement, though during one wet season this number increased to about 350.

Figure 5.2
An Econo Hut, one of the first types of dwellings built for Aboriginal people at Bamyili, Photo G. Jackson

By 1965 Beswick Creek Native Settlement had been re-named Bamyili, and possessed permanent school buildings, a 12-bed hospital with labour ward, a home management centre, laundry and ablution blocks, a brick kitchen/dining unit, an all-weather airstrip, a garage/workshop, and a canteen run by the 'Social Club'. A Welfare Branch publication of the time, stated:

> The advancement of these people is naturally hindered by the old traditional way of life in which the elders of the tribe are the most important and dominant factors. Today the people are gradually emerging from that life eager to take their place among white Australians on an equal footing. Perhaps the easiest way for the reader to see this emergence is to study the ways in which they are managing to adopt types of organisations which we accept as normal in a European community.[14]

As part of this drive the Welfare Branch established a village council, social and sports club, parents and friends' association, adult education classes in 'cookery, civics, mechanics, and social activities' and a youth club, membership of which was dependent upon a 'required standard of behaviour and dress'. However, Aboriginal people's living conditions did not allow the easy attainment of these high standards of dress. Even in the late 1960s the predominant housing for Aboriginal people at Bamyili and Beswick was the 'superior shelter type', a single-room construction of aluminium. Containing neither bathrooms nor kitchens, these dwellings were hardly designed to provide minimum standards of access to health, hygiene or housing. Victor Hood's memories of the time emphasise continuity with the lives Aboriginal people had led at other settlements, especially at Tandangal:

> They sat down at that place, now. Nanny goat, they walk him again. Quiet one, for milk, for tea or kids drinking. That milk, they used to boil him. They eat that nanny goat, too. Nothing, they all gone, now. They used to look after him, feed him, take him out, bring him back la afternoon, milk him. Bamyili. That same copper, same tea [as at Tandangal], count the tea, again. Damper. Outside, no house. Water, no tap. Cart him up [from the creek], that water. Make him big soup, bullocky, sometime nanny goat – they kill him, too, make him soup.[15]

During this period the lives of Aboriginal people became structured in such a way that their traditional autonomy was replaced with a dependence on European goods and services – but with Aboriginal people supplying the labour that ensured the provision of these services. This is most evident in the systems established for the communal preparation and cooking of food. Ronnie Buck describes daily life at Bamyili as follows:

> The kitchen was close by where the shop is now. Twice a day we had meals, breakfast and dinner, lunch I mean. For dinner you had to go back and your family made that dinner. Breakfast was at seven o'clock and lunch at twelve. We used to have our own tea at camp at night. Mainly just the damper that was given to us for the ration.
>
> Breakfast was Weetbix and porridge, that's all. Lunch a chunk of meat mainly with vegetables like potato or boiled pumpkin. You had to be in line to make sure that you did not miss out. You got your plate, knife and fork, and then they served you. Then you eat and got up, grabbed tea or milk.
>
> You had to make sure that you took back the plate and put it in the right place. Not many really liked that sort of food. Half the time, ones like my father went hunting for kangaroo or goanna, when they had time off. Now we realise that some food is good, other food is not good. You are eating rubbish stuff. Then, you just ate what they gave you. You had to eat it or go hungry.
>
> Welfare was taking control over us. We had no say because we didn't know. A person had to do what they said.[16]

In spite of the control that Europeans had over various aspects of their daily lives it is clear that many senior Aboriginal people today remember 'government time' with a degree of fondness. Certainly, life during this period had a sense of purpose, as is evident in the memories of Peter Manabaru:

> Government time. Good thing. Number one. I was working for cooking, then after sometime driving motorcar, truck, operating bulldozer, tractor for farmer. I used to grow a lot of good garden. Sometimes, I used to work for piggery farm and poultry farm for eggs and look after the chooks really good way, and that garden. Grow cabbage and turnips, rockmelon, watermelon, tomato, all sorts of vegetables. Teach all the young blokes to look after that incubator for the little chook. I used to put all them baby chooks on stage. I used to work a lot of weekends, Saturday and Sunday. One person worked one week piggery and one worked poultry. We used to get paid a lot of money but [if you worked] Saturday and Sunday you got [the equivalent of] $900.
>
> They bin have a good time. They cooked their own tucker. We used to work at that kitchen. I used to work at that kitchen, cooking. That proper tucker for that baby. We made good soup, everything. When we rang the bell they come up, their own mother feed them, every 3 o'clock. Milk, soup, custard.

> The cook did all the job for them. There was a sister working there all the time, government time. That nurse, sister, him come down because him want to know if that food all right. Working proper way. No more rubbish way. That nurse say . . .
>
> In government day we bin feed them properly way. We bin working in that kitchen, but we bin taking orders from sisters. If the kids sick, that's our problem. We bin having mununga working there. Him only just foreman, boss man, you know. That man tell me 'you boss'. They'd say 'we want that man' because I used to do a good job for piccaninny.[17]

The first village council was formed in 1961 with the aim of facilitating the exchange of views between 'staff' (non-Aboriginal people) and 'residents' (Aboriginal people). The constitution of the council can be interpreted in terms of the interplay of power relations between these two groups. The council originally consisted of six people who were nominated by residents and in line with Aboriginal knowledge systems and power structures, the six elected councilors were all senior men. However, this position proved to be unsatisfactory from an administrative point of view and in 1965 three young men were nominated to the council by the white staff and were given voting powers equal to those of the senior men.[18] This was an administrative ploy to replace the traditional Aboriginal power structure – in which knowledge is held by senior people – with a European structure, in which knowledge is in the hands of younger, literate people. The council did not become a community-elected body until 1973.[19]

The Assimilation Myth

The myth of assimilation was that it would bring about true equality between Aboriginal and non-Aboriginal people. But it is clear from the way that the policies were implemented that equality was never the intention. Aboriginal people were 'encouraged' to compete with Europeans on an equal basis – but were provided intrinsically unequal access to power, services and resources. Assimilation policies were marred by essential flaws and contradictions, the most flagrant of which is that their implementation was based on the assumption of ongoing Aboriginal inequality, rather than the attainment of comparable skills and an equal standard of living. Moreover, these policies assumed that Aboriginal people would want to embrace a European lifestyle, that they agreed with white people's estimation of Aboriginal culture and values.

Assimilation policies channeled the development of Aboriginal people in specific directions and were structured in such a way that they limited Aboriginals' employment options. It was intended that Aboriginal people would take their place in the European world, but it was always assumed – and perhaps planned – that this place should be subservient to that of Europeans. Aboriginal people were trained only for employment in areas that Europeans considered to be appropriate and placed Aboriginal people in very specific class and gender roles. The Bamyili School, for instance, trained boys in 'manual trades' and girls in 'home management', and in addition, the hospital trained women to be 'nursing assistants, ward-maids and laundry-maids' while men had the opportunity to learn building construction, pig and poultry husbandry, 'the skills of vegetable and fruit production' and other manual tasks.

Thus, such a system of training and employment assigned Aboriginal people to tasks with limited intellectual scope, irrespective of individual abilities or status within their community. Europeans judged ability by European standards and so literacy was a prerequisite for employment in an administrative capacity or other positions of authority. The later history of the settlement would show this to apply only to Europeans. During 'government time', the system was such that the most able and intelligent of Aboriginal people could aspire only to menial, largely physical, achievements within the European sphere. For instance, Jack Chadum – an intelligent and knowledgeable man who in later years became a cultural leader – was commended in a Welfare Branch[20] report as having 'shown great interest and progress during his four years attending the poultry, and is able to grade eggs, care for the poultry, tend the incubator, and keep records of egg production'.

So the assimilation myth served two chief purposes. First, it assuaged any fears that Europeans had concerning the methods used in implementing the policy, the removal of children from their Aboriginal families, for example. Second, it acted to normalise the enormous differences in socio-economic status that existed between Aboriginal and non-Aboriginal people. However, at no stage during the period of assimilation did an Aboriginal child have the same opportunities as its non-Aboriginal counterpart, irrespective of whether that child was born in an urban, rural or remote area of the country. The failure of Aboriginal people to achieve equality – and thereby proving the inherent superiority of Europeans – was built into the system. This, in turn, reinforced the right of Europeans to continue to make decisions which controlled not only the day-to-day lives but also the futures of Aboriginal people.

Six

The Struggle for Culture

My son, him different. Him got to be culture law man, not mununga law man.

(Peter Manabaru's father, circa 1951)

The history of contact between Aboriginal and European Australians has been a history of struggle over culture. The most insidious and extended assault upon Aboriginal culture came with the second phase of the Australian government's assimilation policy. Assimilation proved to be more damaging to Aboriginal people than protectionism had been because it was consciously aimed at annihilating Aboriginal culture. It was concerned with governing Aboriginal people's spiritual and cultural beliefs as well as their physical movements; with controlling their minds as well as their bodies. As such, assimilation policy can be interpreted as a form of cultural genocide. Writing in 1944, the Polish jurist Raphael Lemkin argued that genocide typically consists of two phases, the first of these being the destruction of the cultural and social life of the oppressed group and the second the imposition of the national pattern of the oppressor. Both of these phases are apparent in the implementation of assimilation policies by governments in countries such as Australia, the United States of America, Canada and New Zealand.

There were three main ways by which the Australian government attempted to assimilate Aboriginal people into mainstream European society. The first was by discouraging ceremonial life and traditional systems of thought and by getting Aboriginal people to participate in 'a planned programme of social development' which inculcated the values and practices of European society. The second was by educating Aboriginal children within a Western system of knowledge, and the third way was by removing children of mixed descent from Aboriginal communities and placing them in institutions or with adoptive parents. These, then, were the arenas in which the struggle for culture was played out.

A Planned Programme of Social Development

The principle advocate for assimilation policies in the Northern Territory was the Federal government's Minister for Territories, Paul Hasluck. While he failed to consult Aboriginal people about their own wishes for the future, he did recognise that these policies would be most effectively implemented if Aboriginal people themselves wanted to bring about changes:

> The other great opportunity and responsibility we have is to do something that will give them an interest in making this change themselves. You cannot pour individuals into a mould. Some of these people – and every honourable member who knows the problem will agree with me on this – are going to wait for generations before the old tie of the bush, the tie of the tribal law, the tie of tribal kinship, is loosed sufficiently for them to come our way. We have to be patient, in those cases, for generations.

At a local level, Hasluck's view is echoed in the 1961 report by the Welfare Branch on the Beswick Aboriginal Reserve, which outlines the assimilation mission in terms of community management:

> One may say that the settlement is no longer a place at which merely the bodily needs of natives are catered for. A planned programme of social development is attempted there, the purpose of which is to try to influence and train the individual so that he/she and/or his/her children will be able to participate in everyday Australian life.
>
> . . . perhaps its enormity as a social undertaking will be recognised, and particularly so once it has been pointed out that the major initial problem to be grappled with is that of upsetting the Australian aborigine's entire social tradition, of long standing, which aims deliberately at disencouraging individualism. This traditionalism has its roots in the knowledge, acquired over thousands of years, that the survival of a tribe living under northern Australia's climatic conditions must not be hazarded against the luxury of individualism within the tribe. The European social environment by contrast sets up as an ideal to be sought for (equally deliberately) a spirit of competition between individuals.[1]

Ceremonial Life

Given the presumption of cultural superiority upon which assimilation policy was based, it was inevitable that Aboriginal ceremonial life would be a focus of conflict. This was a struggle in which neither side gained outright victory. While Aboriginal people did not have the power to stop non-Aboriginal people from desecrating their sacred objects, non-Aboriginal people did not have the power to stop Aboriginal people from re-creating those objects. Beswick station was declared an Aboriginal Reserve in 1953, at a time when assimilation policy was in full swing. In line with this policy, the management of the station actively discouraged Aboriginal ceremonial life, which was thought to undermine the 'absorption' of Aboriginal people into a European system of values and way of life. This belief is communicated to the general public in the Australian government publication *Fringe Dwellers*:[2]

> Many aspects of the tribal life of aborigines tend to persist and become barriers to the advancement and eventual assimilation of individuals and of groups.

According to the documentation which has survived, and the oral accounts of Aboriginal people, it seems that ceremonial life at Beswick station was actively discouraged to a greater degree than at other places in the region. The continued flourishing of this life was an on-going concern that was articulated by several of the station managers. There were mixed feelings towards anthropologists at this time, and a feeling among administrators that anthropological interest in Aboriginal culture was somehow contrary to the successful implementation of assimilation policies. For instance, Senior Education Officer L.R. Newby suspected that visits by the renowned Sydney anthropologist A.P. Elkin constituted an illicit strengthening of Aboriginal cultural values and a concomitant breaking down of the European work ethic. Newby's fears were outlined in his December 1953 report to the Acting Director of Native Affairs:

> It seemed to me that tribal ceremonial activity has been intensifying at Beswick. The 'old men' have interfered with efforts to keep young men at work. As far as I could see, further ceremonies were planned and would drain away for varying periods at some time or other almost all the men on the place. I was told that one series was being arranged for

> Professor Elkin. I wondered whether Professor Elkin and party's last visit had contributed to the resurgence of ceremonial life. This was reflected in the variation in the number of natives on the station, from 134 on 1st November to 205 at the end of the month.[3]

This was not the isolated concern of a single station manager, and later Superintendent Bowden pointed out 'the undesirable features arising from the holding of the "Big Sunday" corroborees'.[4] Senior Aboriginal people today recall a different station manager, Superintendent Morey, intentionally burning the bough shelters they erected during preparations for a major ceremony. They were powerless to stop him, but he was powerless to stop them re-erecting them in another place at another time.

In order to counteract the influence of traditional culture, European administrators devised recreational and sporting activities for young Aboriginal people. That this was a strategy for undermining Aboriginal culture, rather than simply a way of increasing the quality of Aboriginal lives, is made clear in Newby's report:

> Reference has already been made to the amount of tribal ceremonial activity. To compensate for and, if possible, to arrest this trend, recreational activities should be arranged for adolescents and young men and women. The young men have purchased a football which they play almost every afternoon. A site for a football ground is being cleared.[5]

The wet season provided an annual buffer for station-dwelling Aboriginal people, as it was more difficult to carry out extended pastoral work during this time of year. On properties such as Mainoru station this was the time when Aboriginal people 'went bush' and held major ceremonies, strengthening and passing on their cultural beliefs. At times it was difficult for people working on stations to join in the ceremonies, which no doubt constituted a potential disruption to the normal rhythm of station life. Minnie George remembers:

> We only just got rations but we didn't have a holiday, nothing. We had to work through the Wet. No holidays, early days. Ceremony time we knocked off. When we were going to make a young man we knocked off, went to the ceremony and went back again to that job afterwards. All the time, never spell.[6]

Not all Europeans in the region believed in cultural genocide. Jack McKay, who owned Mainoru station during the 1950s, did not try to prevent ceremonial activity continuing at its old rhythm. Nellie Camfoo recalled that:

> Every night we play about digeridoo and teach the young ones dance for sacred corroboree and young little kid to make young man you know. The McKays never used to care. If we wanted to finish off sacred way out from station, old Jack used to give us motor car and take us mob down there and leave us. When we finish corroboree he used to come down and check up and pick us up and go back to work. Not wet season but cold weather time too. That Jack been really know about our life. Him the only first one been savvy [understand] us mob life, what we doing. Aboriginal dancing and all that.[7]

Figure 6.1
Women dancing Djarrada, Mainoru station
MAGNT, PIC 047, Dodd Collection

Despite on-going incursions by Europeans, Aboriginal ceremonial life in this region appears to have continued relatively unhampered during the 1960s and 1970s. Major changes had occurred by this time, however, and some important ceremonies were enacted less frequently than before. In 1971, the anthropologist Ken Maddock, who conducted extensive fieldwork in this region during this period, stated that 'of the three extant cults, only the Jubuduruwa is regularly performed'.[8] Elsewhere, Maddock observed that few nights passed without some corroboree singing, though dancing was less common:[9]

> The majority of Beswick Aborigines are not only living outside their country, but have little or no first hand knowledge of it, they know the names of many of its waters and landmarks, but rarely if ever revisit it . . . Despite their linguistic diversity, they perform close variants of the same ceremonies and have a similar social organisation. These groups – Dalabon (or Ngalbon), Rembarnga, Maiali (or Gunwinggu), Djauan, Gunei, Mangarai, Jargman and fragments, often of uncertain tribal affiliation from Roper Mission – maintain a flourishing ceremonial and cult life. They do not exclude one another from ritual performances.

As Maddock observed, ceremonial activity was characterised by cooperation rather than competition between groups. The make-up of the community at this time was diverse. The relative proportion of language groups living at Beswick Aboriginal Reserve in 1961 is recorded in Table 6.1[10] and was little changed at the end of the decade.[11]

Language Group	**% of Population**
Jawoyn	17
Mielli	25
Ngalkbun	35
Rembarrnga	13
Mara and others	10
Total	100

Table 6.1
Language Groups, Beswick Aboriginal Reserve, 1961

From a European viewpoint, the high proportion of people from other language groups in Jawoyn country set the stage for conflict between these groups, Instead, what arose was cooperation in order to ensure continuity in core cultural practices. This is evident in the fact that while the Ngalkpon formed the most numerous language group during this period, there is no indication in any of the documentation or oral histories of the time that the control of the land passed from Jawoyn hands. Rather than taking over Jawoyn land, Ngalkpon people became the custodians for

Jawoyn traditional owners. Maddock's conclusions in this regard are enlightening:

> Similarity in social and ceremonial forms has evidently offset the clan and tribal splintering and the diversity of languages, and so enabled a new type of life to emerge in which Aboriginal tradition continues modified and truncated in a context of sedentary settlement, money economy, use of English, acquisition of manufactured goods, pursuit of European-type pastimes, education in schools, acceptance of monogamy, birth and death in hospitals and incipient political consciousness of themselves as Aborigines having interests and values in common with Aborigines throughout the Northern Territory.[12]

Schooling

Formal schooling was essential to the programme of social development and education that was the cornerstone of assimilation policy. The first such in the Barunga–Wugularr region was located at Tangandal settlement and in some ways marked the beginning of a sustained incursion upon Indigenous belief systems in the area. The school was established in 1951, partly in response to demands from Aboriginal people in the Northern Territory for better access to European education for their children. A strike in 1947 by Aboriginals in Darwin had brought this issue into the public consciousness, prompting the Northern Territory administration to be seen to act on this issue. But the other force behind the establishment of the Tangandal school was the role of education in the successful implementation of assimilation policies.

In March 1951, Mr Allom took up the position as Head Teacher of the newly established Beswick Native School. He found that most school-aged children were not living at Beswick station but were at Tangandal, eight miles away. Mr Allom decided to live in a tent at Tangandal and establish the school there. He built an open-air classroom consisting of a small piece of canvas and leafy boughs. It must have been reasonably successful since up to 40 children attended the Tangandal school while between four and seven additional children living at Beswick station were taught by an assistant teacher. Though there were white children living at Beswick they were not allowed to attend the new school. Schooling, like other aspects of assimilation policy, was marked by segregation rather than integration, as indicated in this report by Senior Education Officer Newby:

> Attendance at Native Schools might have serious effects on the emotional and social development of white children and, consequently, on their intellectual development. There are a number of white children at Beswick. Although there can be no thought of their attending the Native School at the present time I advised their parents to allow their children to continue with correspondence work in their homes.[13]

The establishment of a school at Tangandal created an unprecedented dilemma for local Aboriginal people and the manner in which they reacted depended on how they envisaged their children's futures. Some people saw European education as an essential tool for living in what they feared was increasingly becoming a 'white man's world'. They felt that European education could act as a means of freeing Aboriginal people from the domination of white bosses and so encouraged their children to attend the school. Others were concerned that the European system of education would undermine their children's traditional beliefs and understandings. Peter Manabaru's father fitted into this category and he did not allow Peter to attend the school. Instead, Peter went to the 'bush school' of Aboriginal people.

> They used to call my daddy 'culture man'. They had to call him first before ceremonies. I was only one kid hanging around there. I stayed there because my father was working there. My father didn't want me to go to school.
>
> I went to that mununga school for one week. I bin like that school all right but my father didn't want me to stay. He want me to learn culture. My father didn't want me to go to school. He used to tell me himself: 'What you like, mununga school or blackfella school?' Now, I liked mununga school but he didn't want me to go. I might forget about my culture. That policeman asked him [to send me]. That manager asked him. That government man asked him. He said 'No, that's your way. I've got to send him to my school. My son, him different. Him got to be culture law man, not mununga law man'.[14]

As his father had wished, Peter grew up to become a culture law man. Though unable to read or write, he is a very powerful man within the present-day Barunga community – and that power comes from his knowledge of Aboriginal culture. Others chose to send their children to school and their children gained a better understanding of European systems and so were empowered in those ways. What is clear, however, is that there was considerable pressure on Aboriginal people to send their children to the European school and whether or not people did so was an important cultural choice. The kind of pressure exerted is evident in the recollections of Minnie George, who went to school at Roper River Mission but ran away to Barunga:

> We used to play hiding and run away from school in the bush. We'd drop down dress, put on cockrag and go. . . . And that other policeman came with his missus. That missus brought a tin of lollies. She was carrying them. We were looking at her from the hill. She was following us with that lolly . . . Those two had been hunting everywhere for us to take us back to school. But we didn't want it. We wanted bush. They wanted us to wear clothes but we chucked them out and wore cockrag . . . We didn't like that teacher. He was a cheeky one. We called him 'School Master'. He belted us no more little bit. We cried and cried. No matter how much they took us back we still ran away.[15]

School was important to the implementation of assimilation policies not only for the information the children were taught but also because the schooling system itself inculcated European values, formally introducing and reinforcing values essential to the planned transition of Aboriginal children to a European workplace. Among these values were respect for the authority of the state, obedience, the desirability of clothing, the merit of work and an acceptance of the scheduling of one's time by others. The importance placed on such cultural values is evident in the operation of the school established at Mainoru station by Jack McKay's sister, Mrs Dodd. For instance, one of Mrs Dodd's self-imposed responsibilities was overseeing Aboriginal women sewing clothing for the children. Mrs Dodd envisaged her role as part of a wider crusade that was the duty of all Europeans: that of civilising the native. As Cowlishaw[16] points out 'clothing the black bodies was a crucial task'. Largely on the basis of the social aspects of her work, Mrs Dodd's school was applauded by government authorities. Patrol Officer Ryan reported:

> Mainoru station is unique and outstanding for its attention paid to the school children and pre-school children . . . From 7 am until 8 pm on seven days a week the bulk of the children are in or adjacent to the station homestead. Not only do they receive excellent academic training but the attention paid to their general well being is most creditable.[17]

Figure 6.2
First days at Mainoru School
MAGNT PH047, Dodd Collection

Figure 6.3
Mrs Dodd teaching children at Mainoru School. Jeanette McDonald and Glen Stuart (now Wesan) in front row. Jill Curtis in middle row centre.
MAGNT PH047, Dodd Collection

Rocky Cameron attended the Mainoru school during the 1950s. His memories focus on the discipline the children received, which would have been quite a shock after the freedom of camp life, and the provision of regular food:

We went to that school all the time. That school is where we learnt English. I was really brainy with Maths. I could multiply and add up in my head. I didn't have to put it down in a book. I bin savvy the times tables right through to 12 times – if I asked these kids today 12x12, they wouldn't know. We used to start school about 7am in the morning. If we were naughty we couldn't knock off until 6 o'clock at night. Fair dinkum.

We used to go to school, come out for tea, have milk – not this powdered milk, goat's milk – go to the toilet, wash our hands, back into school. Never allowed to play around. Same during lunch hour, just lunch, toilet, wash your hands, back into the class. They used to mix that goat milk with vitamins. That goat gave good milk and good meat. It's better than lamb, not so much fat. The old people used to look after the goats. In the morning we had bread and milk and at lunchtime we had bread and vegemite, no meat. Mrs Dodd used to mix that vegemite herself, stir it in a big bucket, enough for the whole class.

Figure 6.4
Group from Mainoru school in Darwin under the Hasluck banner, won by Abie Lawrence and Lorna Martin (holding banner) for 'discipline, dress and deportment'
MAGNT PH047, Dodd Collection

That's the hardest way I ever learnt. If they gave you something and you didn't say 'Thank you', you got the strap for that. If you wanted to go to the toilet, you had to put up your hand, not just run out. You had to ask permission to do what you wanted to do. That was a hard school. The teacher used the cane across our palm or our legs. She used that feather duster, that cane, sometimes a two-foot ruler or a leather strap. This was a hard time for us. It's better, now. That was a rough time. My parents knew about those hidings but they wouldn't say anything. Mrs Dodd was a really good teacher but she gave too many hidings.

If we didn't turn up for school a copper would come and look for us. One time the whole school walked out, those kids were sick and tired of getting hidings, and the policeman had to come up from Maranboy and look for us. We wouldn't even say 'boo' to the teacher. You'd get a hiding for that. You had to say 'May I go to the toilet?' not 'Can I go to the toilet?' Not can, may. If we were sleepy Mrs Dodd would get a bucket of cold water and chuck it on us to wake us up. Mrs Dodd used to take us down the river for a bogie [swim]. That water pump never used to work. There was no hot water, nothing, even in cold weather you had to jump in the river.

In those days there was no video, no tapes, nothing. Only the old gramophone, with the needle. That Mrs Dodd had one. She took it to the school sometimes. On Saturdays we used to walk around picking up papers, just for tea and sugar, no bread, no beef. In 1965 my family left that teacher and we walked to Maningrida. I went to Bamiyli school, too, and later I went to Koomilda in Darwin. We went to the Sports Carnival in Darwin, too, under that [Paul] Hasluck banner, that flag.[18]

The Achilles Heel of Assimilation

The Achilles heel of assimilation was the unquestioned assumption of European superiority, which prevented Europeans from trying to learn what Aboriginal people wanted for their own future. Convinced of the inherent correctness of their own lifestyles and cultural values, they did not think to consult Aboriginal people about their own plans and desires. They failed to ask the obvious question: 'Would you like to be like us?' Had they done so they would have received an answer along the lines of, 'We would like to have regular food and some of your material goods, but we don't want our children to grow up to be like white people. We want them to grow up as Aboriginal people.'

While Aboriginal people recognised that many of their actions were controlled by Europeans, in no way did they accept European notions of cultural superiority. Assimilation was resisted vigorously by elders in the Barunga–Wugularr region, not only because they valued their own culture but also because they did not accept the cultural values and mores of mainstream European society. This resistance was recognised by the European administrators:

> These systems of thought are in most crucial respects incompatible as active social systems – one can not live with the other on a 'give and take' basis. The traditional native view of correct social behaviour

> cannot be reconciled with the white man's and the latter's system is consequently opposed most strenuously by the elders ('the traditionalists'), both men and women, and to some degree by many others.[19]

The struggle for culture did not have a clear-cut victor. Aboriginal lifestyles did change during the period that assimilation policies were in place, but these changes were largely in the economic sphere where there are highly visible, quantifiable indicators such as houses, cars and shops. The continuity in social and cultural values was less visible and the changes that occurred in them were much more difficult to identify, much less quantify.

Continuity in Aboriginal cultural practices in the Barunga–Wugularr region denied the central assumption of assimilation, that Aboriginal people would want to take on European cultural values. The impetus for Aboriginal resistance to assimilation lay with Aboriginal people's respect for their own system of cultural values – they were repelled by the assumption that they would wish to become the same as white people. They did not agree with a cultural ideology in which material objects were valued above spiritual or religious knowledge and they did not wish to replace their communal values with the individualistic values of European society. Nor did they desire to adopt a European work ethic that would decrease the time they could spend with their family and lower the quality of their day-to-day lives. They did not wish to prepare themselves to leave behind their traditional lands and take their place as servants to white people in the 'wider community'. Assimilation failed because Aboriginal people did not wish to be Europeans.

Seven

The Stolen Generations

I suppose they thought education would compensate but it didn't. Education doesn't replace the hurt and not having a mother and not having a family. I'm not better off because I missed out on the most important things. We missed out on our culture and our family. Nothing can replace that.

Eileen Cummings, 2001

The removal of children of mixed descent from their Aboriginal families was a particularly devastating technique used to implement the assimilation policy and was carried out systematically throughout the Australian States and Territories for periods ranging from 60 to 120 years. It affected many generations of Aboriginal people and its effects were disastrous – not only for the children themselves, but their families and communities also. The children who were removed are known as the 'Stolen Generations', a phrase coined in a seminal article published by Peter Read in 1981.[1] The Stolen Generations serve as a powerful symbol of the harm done to Aboriginal people by Europeans.

The forcible removal of children was included in the definition of genocide adopted in the United Nations 1948 Convention on the Prevention and Punishment of the Crime of Genocide. The Secretary General pointed out that the removal of children from their parents forced upon those children 'at an impressionable and receptive age a culture and mentality different from their parents. This process tends to bring about the disappearance of the group as a cultural unit in a relatively short time'.[2] The Venezuelan delegate to the General Assembly argued that:

> The forced transfer of children to a group where they would be given an education different from that of their own group, and would have new customs, a new religion and probably a new language, was in

> practice tantamount to the destruction of their group, whose future depended on that generation of children. Such transfer might be made from a group with a low standard of civilisation . . . to a highly civilised group . . . yet if the intent of the transfer were the destruction of the group, a crime of genocide would undoubtedly have been committed.[3]

Viewed in tandem with the contemporary assumption that 'full-blood' Aboriginal people were dying out, the separation of children of mixed descent from their Aboriginal families can be interpreted as a form of cultural genocide. The practices and policies that resulted in the removal of these children by 'compulsion, duress or undue influence' are traced in the Australian government publication *Bringing them Home. The National Inquiry into the Separation of Aboriginal and Torres Strait Islander Children from their Families.*[4] This inquiry found that the major components of forcible removal were:

- Deprivation of liberty by detaining children and confining them in institutions.
- Abolition of parental rights by taking the children and by making children wards of the Chief Protector or Aborigines Protection Board or by assuming custody and control.
- Abuses of power in the removal process.
- Breach of guardianship obligations on the part of the Protectors, Protection Boards and other 'carers'.

From 1863 until 1911 the Northern Territory was annexed to South Australia and its people subject to South Australian laws. During this period, the statutory basis for the removal of children from their Aboriginal homes was laid out in the *Ordinance for the Protection, Maintenance and Upbringing of Orphans and Other Destitute Children and Aborigines Act*, 1844. When the Northern Territory gained self-administration, this ordinance was replaced by the *Aborigines Act* of 1910 and, later, by the *Aboriginals Ordinance* of 1936. Under this legislation, the Chief Protector, later the Director of Native Welfare, was the legal guardian of every Aboriginal and 'half-caste' child, notwithstanding that the child had a parent or other relative living. Under these laws, the Chief Protector had the power to remove Aboriginal half-caste children under the age of 18 years from their homes and to take on guardianship responsibilities for these children. Similar legislation was passed in every state in Australia, setting the statutory framework for separations nation-wide. This process was not confined to Australia, however, and comparable legislation was enacted in countries such as New Zealand, the United States of America and Canada.[5]

Why Separate Children from Their Families?

In examining the removal of children of mixed descent from their families, the first question that arises is motivation. Why would a government want to separate children from their families? What could be so important that it motivated the state to implement a systematic programme of taking young children away from their parents and incurring the expense of placing them in foster homes or rearing them in institutional care?

There are many complex answers to this question. Cowlishaw[6] argues that it was the logical development of two wider social programmes: increasing state intervention in the affairs of poor families and the logic of racial categorisation. The convergence of these two programs identified a series of racial categories for social intervention programs. A plethora of racial distinctions was made by Europeans at the time, including 'half-castes', 'quadroons', 'octaroons' and even categories such as 'half Asian/half Aboriginal'. The removal of children was based purely on racial heritage, with skin colour being taken to be the external indicator of this heritage. While there are parallels with the removal of children from poor families in Britain, the difference in the case of Aboriginal people is that the removal of their children was legislated for simply on the grounds of race. The outcome was that around one in six or seven Aboriginal children was removed from the family in comparison to one in three hundred non-Aboriginal children.[7]

An important impetus for the removal of children in the Northern Territory, in particular, was a fear that the white population could be over-run by Aboriginal people of mixed descent. At best, it was thought that these people would constitute an idle and impoverished underclass existing on the periphery of the mainstream and at worst, that they might present a future threat to the state. As Austin[8] points out, there was a sense that 'their supposedly superior White ancestry rendered Half Castes more capable of acts of resistance to the settlers and of assuming a leadership role in such action'. This concern was made very clear in the discussion at the 1937 conference of Commonwealth and State Aboriginal Authorities. The problem is outlined in the memorandum presented to the conference by Professor Cleland, Chairman of the Advisory Council of Aborigines, South Australia:

> The number of half-castes in certain parts of Australia is increasing, not as a result of additional influx of white blood, but following on inter-marriage amongst themselves, where they are living under protected conditions, such as at the Government aboriginal stations at Point Pearce and Point McLeay, in South Australia. This may be the beginning of a possible problem of the future. *A very unfortunate situation would arise if a large half-caste population breeding within themselves eventually arose in any of the Australian States.* It seems to me that there can only be one satisfactory solution to the half-caste problem, and that is the ultimate absorption of these persons in the white population.[9] [italics added]

At this time the Aboriginal population of the Northern Territory outnumbered the non-Aboriginal population by a ratio of almost five to one. There were around 19,000 Aboriginal people and only 4,000 people of European and Asian origin. This disparity was exacerbated by substantive differences between the birth rates of Aboriginal and non-Aboriginal people, calculated by Dr C.E. Cook, Chief Protector of Aboriginals, Northern Territory, as 18 per 1,000 for Aboriginals and –0.3 for non-Aboriginals. Cook expressed the Territory's dilemma in the following terms:

> If aborigines are protected physically and morally, before long there will be in the Northern Territory, a black race, already numbering around 19,000, and multiplying at a rate far in excess of that of the whites. If we leave them alone, they will die, and we shall have no problem, apart from dealing with those pangs of conscience which must attend the passing of a neglected race. If, on the other hand, we protect them with the elaborate measures of protection which every conscientious protector would adopt, we shall raise another problem which may become a serious one from a national viewpoint, for we shall have in the Northern Territory, and possibly in North-western Australia also, a large black population which may drive out the white.
>
> The policy of the Commonwealth is to do everything possible to convert the half-caste into a white citizen . . . My view is that unless the black population is speedily absorbed into the white, the process will soon be reversed, and in 50 years, or a little later, the white population of the Northern Territory will be absorbed into the black.[10]

Cook's fear that the white population could be absorbed into the black was not without basis, given that at that time there were around five white men in the Territory for every white woman. Moreover, it is clear that Cook's remarks were based on the assumption of the time that full-blood Aboriginal people were destined for extinction. This assumption underpins the second reason the Australian government put so much effort into separating children of mixed descent from their Aboriginal families. Ostensibly humanitarian, the incentive was that the best future for those children would be to help them adopt the 'superior' lifestyle of white Australians, entailing eschewing the 'backward' practices of a decadent and dying people and taking on the vocations, values and customs of white citizens. Thus, if the government could achieve its plan to convert half-castes into white citizens it solved two problems: not only did it neutralise the potential threat of large populations of people with Aboriginal values and allegiances in many parts of the country, it increased the number of people with the skills, habits and cultural values needed for a fast-developing nation. At this time Australia was gearing up to implement a major immigration programme under the pithy and powerful slogan 'populate or perish'. Viewed in this light, the transformation of Aboriginal people of mixed descent into white citizens can be interpreted as a method of populating Australia from within, providing the developing country with a suitably trained workforce.

A third motivation for the removal of Aboriginal children from their families was to save them from their role as social outcasts. This view was based on the assumption that Aboriginal people embraced similar cultural values to Europeans and would reject children of mixed liaisons. Moreover, it was thought that their assimilation into the white mainstream would improve the children's moral standards and, by extension, those of the community. The reasoning behind this is perhaps worth noting. In the Northern Territory, the *Aboriginals Ordinance* of 1936 prohibited a European man from living, cohabiting or having sexual intercourse with any Aboriginal or half-caste woman to whom he was not lawfully married. Marriage between a female Aboriginal and a male non–Aboriginal, however, had to be approved by the Chief Protector, and this approval was extraordinarily difficult to obtain. In tandem, these two provisions effectively made it illegal for

European men and Aboriginal women to have a sexual relationship and children from such relationships became material proof that the law had been broken. Moreover, these children were illegitimate and the rearing of these children by their parents was necessarily in an immoral environment since the children themselves were proof that the parents were law-breakers. The belief that Aboriginal people would not provide the children with suitable moral training was exacerbated by the application of European standards of diet, accommodation and sanitation to the dwellings of Aboriginal people, without having provided those people with the means by which they could improve them. The outcome was that white Australians saw separating children from their Aboriginal families as a humanitarian act, rescuing them from debauched, dirty and backward surroundings and saving them from life as outcasts. This view is evident in Cook's statement:

> Children are removed from the evil influence of the aboriginal camp with its lack of moral training and its risk of serious organic infectious disease. They are properly fed, clothed and educated as white children, they are subjected to constant medical supervision and in receipt of domestic and vocational training.[11]

The assessments of administrators and other officials filtered down to ordinary Australians, aided by the popular press and selected government publications such as *Our Aborigines*, produced to educate the wider community in such matters. The view commonly held by white Australians of the time was expressed by Annette Smith:

> How could people like me let it happen? Aboriginal women used to leave their babies because the tribes wouldn't accept half-castes. Sometimes, they used to kill them. The Aboriginal Welfare Board took the children because they were half-white. They weren't full bloods and they weren't wanted by their tribes. The mothers were begging the white townspeople to take them. I can remember reading about one case at Tenterfield, in New South Wales. They took them whether [or not] the tribe and the mothers wanted them to, in some cases, because they weren't being cared for properly. Because the tribe didn't want them, neither did the whites, so the Aboriginal Board stepped in and took them.[12]

To blame the white people who lived during these times is too simple and to understand how people thought during such times is much more difficult. As Peter Read[13] points out, even in the 1960s few people, either white or black, actually understood that there was a policy of removal. To most people, the stories they heard of were individual instances. To them, the frequency with which Aboriginal children featured in such incidents was due to the fact that many Aboriginal people lived in abject conditions and were less able to provide the standards of living that were expected by Europeans. Nevertheless, the question of why people weren't told is an important one, not least because it is important to identify such masking in the present. The confusion and anger of contemporary Australians when made aware of the hiding of such unpleasant histories are addressed by Henry Reynolds in a recent book *Why Weren't we Told?*.[14]

A fourth motivation for removing children of mixed descent from their Aboriginal families, contained in the above statement by Annette Smith, was a fear that some of them might be killed. In terms of Aboriginal people of full descent, this concern was expressed in the following exchange between Mr Neville, Commissioner of Native Affairs, Western Australia, and Mr Harkness, member of the Aborigines Protection Board, New South Wales:

> Mr Neville: The full bloods may be looked after on the cattle stations for the time being, but their number is decreasing rapidly as a result of tribal practices. In a bad season in the north practically no children are reared, while in a good season the number may be fairly considerable. Infanticide and abortion are extensively practised among the bush people. They follow their own customs and no attempt to influence them has much result. We have to consider whether we should allow any race living amongst us to practice the abominations which are prevalent among these people.
>
> Mr Harkness: And do they actually kill them?
>
> Mr Neville: Yes, they just knock them on the head if they cannot feed them.[15]

While this statement was based on a misinformed and gross generalisation, it would be unfair not to mention that some Aboriginal people in the Barunga–Wugularr region did take a dim view of children of mixed descent. Referring to the period around the 1930s and 1940s, Hitler Wood Katcherelli states that:

> A lot of men had a yellafella kid too. We didn't like yellafellas because we didn't like white men. White men didn't like blackfella either. They were shooting blackfellas, taking land, making us speak English. It was really hard, both ways.[16]

In these early days of first contact, some women had to fight for the lives of their light-skinned children, as recounted in the following narrative by Tex Camfoo:

> I was born in the camp.
>
> My mother was Florida. When my sister was born, a couple of days later, they raided our camp and they killed my sister. And my aunty Edna, Niluk, she got me and ran away to the hills with me. In those days when there were half-castes, they used to kill us, you know, because they reckoned we were a different colour to the other Aboriginal people. But my aunty Edna said. 'No, you can't kill this little boy. He's my little boy. And he's going to spear kangaroo and fish and get sugar bag and look after me when he grows up.'[17]

As single instances, such as that of Tex Camfoo's sister, came to the attention of white authorities they were given wide publicity. Then, the individual incident became generalised so that many children were seen as being in physical danger. In fact, such instances were rare and, in some cases, Aboriginal men fought hard to maintain custody of their light-skinned children. George Jangawanga recalls:

> Eileen, my [light-skinned] daughter, used to be a young girl, Eileen Jangawanga, and from Mainoru I went away to Mountain Valley, working. I used to be a bullock tailer, minding bullocks. And that's the time, at Mainoru, that that Mununga [white man] claimed my daughter. And we were going to put her in school. Heather Dodd, Mrs Dodd, and Mr McKay from Mainoru, said they are not allowed to bring me back that kid.
>
> And he's telling me,
>
> 'No, you won't get that piccaninny back. We've got to take that kid,' they were telling me.
>
> 'No, that's my colour, that's not your colour,' I told them.
>
> 'Still, we can't give you,' Jack McKay said, 'because she's half-caste and you are full black Aboriginal.'
>
> I told him,
>
> 'Your sister can't claim. If you claim, you should claim your own

Figure 7.1
George Jangawunga being interviewed by Gary Jackson, near Maranboy, 1991. Joli Laiwongga in the background

> colour. This is my colour,' I told him like that. Well that's the time I went back to Mountain Valley again and I came back with a spear. I thought 'I don't want to let my kid go. I'll have to go and get her back.'
>
> . . . I sat down and by and by I got a spear, woomera and a bundle of spears. I was waiting for them to come down. They came down now, with a little revolver. Sandy McKay came down.
>
> He came in and called me to come here. Then, target like, he shot that drum, and tried to frighten me. He shot low like, bang, and hit that drum.
>
> I didn't move. I stood up to him.
>
> After that I grabbed that somebody and hit him, that man, and chucked the revolver away . . . They had the girl up there at their house and I got her out from there and brought her back.[18]

This incident not only demonstrates how strongly some men were willing to fight to keep their light-skinned children, it shows that people such as George Jangawanga classed children of mixed descent as Aboriginal, rather than European.

The Children's Stories

The National Inquiry into the Separation of Aboriginal and Torres Strait Islander Children from their Families[19] points out the taking of the children from their homes by force and their confinement in institutions 'amounted to deprivation of liberty and, in fact, imprisonment, in the common law sense'. This deprivation of liberty was legislated for by individual states and Territories, directly discriminating on racial grounds. The question that arises concerns how the children were taken from their families. What actually happened? Did the parents give them up? Were they taken on the basis of a mutual agreement between families and the institutions involved or was force or coercion involved? Did the removal process involve abuses of power?

The best way of understanding the experiences of the Stolen Generations is through listening to the children's stories. Here, this is traced primarily through the experiences of two little girls from the Barunga–Wugularr region, Eileen Cummings and Lorraine Siwers, who were stolen on the same day. They would not have realised it at the time, but they lived their infancy under the threat of being stolen. Both recall having been given special treatment by their mothers when they were little. Eileen Cummings remembers:

> Mum worked at the station house. I was with her all the time. I was always there. Jack McKay let me run that place like it was my home. He only sent me down the camp if I was naughty. Most of the time I was there at the station house with Mum.[20]

Lorraine Siwers recalls:

> My sister Bessie says I was Mummy's little girl. She said 'You'd always have the most moiee' [bush plums]. I was spoiled rotten by Mum.[21]

No doubt such special treatment was because these mothers wanted their children's memories of their Aboriginal homes to be sweet. It is hard to imagine the poignancy and tragedy of rearing such children, knowing that they would probably be stolen while barely infants and would live most of their young lives in an institution.

Some mothers dealt with this situation by attempting to have local white people adopt their light-skinned children. While whites interpreted this as the mothers not wanting them, it was an Aboriginal strategy to *keep* the children, not lose them. Knowing that their children were marked for separation, the women reasoned that if local people adopted the children they would still be accessible to their Aboriginal families. For this reason, Eileen Cumming's auntie Alice agreed to Mrs Dodd of Mainoru station adopting her light-skinned daughter Pixie and, in this case, Alice was able to see her child grow up. The same desparate measure was taken by Lorraine Siwer's mother, Judy, but was thwarted by the affection her child held for her:

> Some white people wanted to adopt me. They tried to keep me at Mataranka when I was little but I wouldn't settle. I kept crying. I wanted to go back to the camp. I carried on so much they had to take me back.

> They couldn't separate mum and me. I used to cry if mum went off anywhere, even to the toilet. The white people bought me new clothes but I took them off. I liked the dress Mum made me out of flour bags.[22]

Lorraine's mother must have been both ingenious and determined, as she was able to keep her daughter with her for a remarkable seven years. However, in September 1948 Lorraine and Eileen were stolen. Patrol Officer Ryan of the Native Affairs Branch recorded the collection of these young girls and two other small children as a small incident within a much broader report:

> At 1430 hours we left Beswick Station with a four years old half-caste girl, Rita, and later collected another half-caste girl, Lorrie, at Tandangal. Both these children were left temporarily at Maranboy Police Station . . . [Three days later] I collected the abovementioned two half-caste girls, another half-caste girl, Eileen, and a half-caste boy, Tommy Olsen.[23]

The dispassionate tone of Ryan's report contrasts strongly with the memories of the children who were taken away. As with the violent deaths that occurred in an earlier time, it seems that government officials became involved in a conspiracy of silence. Certainly, the grief experienced by Aboriginal people was rarely included in the reports of the time. Lorraine Siwers recalls:

> I liked living at Tandangal. I can remember the spring there. They used to wash those cheeky yams in the water [to get rid of the poison]. We used to hear the trucks coming and mum and all the ladies would grab all the kids and take off for the hills. My mum used to put me on her shoulders and run . . . I don't why we didn't run that day. Maybe the police got off the truck a few miles out and circled us. My mum used to work in the house for Mr Fraser-Allen and his wife. I used to play with their son. I don't know why they'd do that . . . My mother helped to look after their son, John.
>
> I just saw two men in khaki and they were the ones that came with us on the truck. Mum was trying to hang on to me, pull me, but there was a couple of fellas there putting us in the truck. They were just taking us off our mothers. A lot of them were just screaming. The ladies and old people were by the truck and they were all crying and I asked my mum why she was crying. I said 'Don't worry, Mum. I'm only going for a ride.' I was excited because it was the first time I had been in a truck, but she just kept on crying. Going along the track I

> saw my auntie and uncle looking after nanny goats. I said 'I'm going for a ride. See you when I get back.' I couldn't understand why she [my mother] was crying . . . I never saw my mother again.[24]

Eileen Cummings had been living with her mother and her mother's husband, Chuckerduck, who was head stockman at Mainoru station (see Figure 4.3). She was stolen at the age of four:

> I remember them coming to Mainoru and picking me up in a red truck. I got in the red truck with Mr Sweeney. Mum was there. She was working at the station house and I was jumping up on the fence feeling really good. Then I saw the truck. She didn't know what was happening. What I thought they said was they were going to take me for a ride to Katherine. I thought 'Oh good, I'm going for a ride.' That's what I thought it was. Then all of a sudden when we got away from Mainoru I started to cry, I missed my mum.
>
> I remember her standing there on the steps of the station house looking when the truck pulled up. I don't recall saying goodbye to her or anything. I thought I was just going for a ride. I remember the look on Jack McKay's face, really angry. I recall him saying something like 'You know I don't like this. Children shouldn't be taken away from their mothers.' I was only a little girl.[25]

Such separation was particularly hard on children from communities in the Barunga–Wugularr region. Unable to speak English they could not clearly communicate even simple needs to officials, none of whom spoke Aboriginal languages. This exacerbated the situation, making the children even more frightened than they might otherwise have been. Eileen Cummings recalls:

> When we picked up Tommy he was working in the mine with his father. He was really dirty. When we were driving to Katherine he starting vomiting. He vomited right over Rita's head. He was about the same age as me. As we were driving to Darwin, we were in the back of the truck, crying for our mothers.[26]

Lorraine Siwers recalls:

> I just saw two men in khaki and they were the ones that come with us on the truck. They stood on either corner [of the back of the truck]. When we wanted to go to the toilet they wouldn't stop. I spoke [Aboriginal] language and only a few words of English. Those little kids had to pee right there on the truck.

> When it started to get dark I started worrying 'We should be home, now.' Rita and Tommy and Eileen started crying. Tommy had grease all over him because he had been down a well or a mine or something, maybe to hide him. It was getting dark and I said to them 'I want to go home.' They said something in English. I was talking language to them. Rita and Eileen were crying all the time on the truck and when we got to Bagot. We were all crying, all night. We would have driven the policeman mad that had to look after us.[27]

The distress suffered by these children was in direct violation of the legal responsibility of Protectors to provide for the physical and emotional well being of children who were removed from their parents, since their parents had been denied the opportunity to perform this function for them.[28] As they huddled in the back of the truck, crying and covered in urine and vomit, the trip away from their home must have been a nightmare. When they arrived in town their condition would be physical 'proof' of their neglect at home.

The situation did not improve once they reached Darwin and the children continued to grieve for their families. Seeking their rights to liberty and being brought up by their families, Lorraine and the others tried to find their way back to their parents:

> They were always crying those two little ones [Rita and Eileen], I had to protect them. When I left the old people they had said 'You're the eldest. You've got to look after those little ones.' I think that was why they let me go. We tried to run away in Darwin, when we got to Bagot [Compound]. I had Rita on my hip and Eileen's hand and Tommy and two other girls, Shirley and Tania. We just went through the scrub and they must have found us missing and those men in khaki came again. They just took us back to Darwin. 'We were going home,' we said.[29]

Growing Up in an Institution

The institutionalisation of children such as Eileen, Rita and Lorraine was a key component of the Australian government's assimilation policy, providing the means by which these children could be inculcated in the values of the dominant society. The way in which this was implemented conforms to the second phase of genocide as defined by Raphael Lemkin: that of imposing the national pattern of the oppressor. Denied the cultural and social lives into which they had been born, the stolen children were now to be educated into the customs, religion and language of the dominant society.

One of the major ways in which the state's rearing of stolen children differed from that of their parents is in the belief systems and cultural values that were taught to the children. They were taught to be ashamed of their Aboriginal identities and were denied access to their birth languages and cultures. As Eileen Cummings states:

> They took us completely, isolated us, changed our names, took us as far as they could from our country and our people.[30]

The active denial of their Indigenous identity and attempts to replace this with white, middle-class values, is demonstrated in the following description by Lorraine Siwers:

> They were too ashamed and hid us away on Croker Island. There were so many of us. Sometimes the station hand would offer to adopt them, maybe take over their daughter. When we got to Croker they told us not to talk language. They said 'You kids got to talk English from now on' and they told us not to have anything to do with the Aborigines on Croker. Rita and Eileen and I would sit in a circle and we'd talk language. We'd say 'We don't like that lady' or 'We want to go home', until we gradually forgot. They'd yell at us if they caught us, before we got the nice lady, Sister Betty Knowles. She was really good. She didn't give us a hiding or anything, whereas some of the others did give us a hiding. I probably knew a little bit of English. When I went back the old people would say 'You talk proper language, not this Kriol.'
>
> The Aborigines on Croker Island used to have corroboree and play the didgeridoo. We'd hear them and get excited and sometimes we'd start crying for home. All the other kids talked in their language, too.
>
> We'd go to church all the time. Wednesday we had devotions and church Sunday morning and night. The pictures on Friday night, cowboy ones. One year they showed us 'A Tale of Two Cities'. We thought that was really good. We were all crying all the time. They kept that for a week and we saw it over and over. We had cartoons, too. We saw pictures of big cities, Sydney or Adelaide, something new. Then I came down to the Christian convention, that's why I wanted to come to Adelaide when they were sending kids to different states, when they were going to close Croker.[31]

The popularity of *A Tale of Two Cities* is not surprising, given that its subject matter was oppression and wrongful imprisonment. Christianity is sometimes identified as a major factor in the assimilation process, but the inculcation of Christian values was only one, albeit powerful, focus of assimilation policies. Many of these children may have learnt Christian values in their home communities, too, but in such cases they would have been appended to Aboriginal cultural and religious values. For the stolen children, this core of Indigenous identity was denied and, as the above description shows, European values were surreptitiously instilled through the use of media such as films and cartoons, as well as by more overt teachings.

One of the fundamental arguments for taking these children from their families was that it was for 'their own good'. But what constitutes 'good'? Did the children receive the standard of living and education that they were promised? Did they receive equal treatment to that given to white children living in institutions at that time? The National Inquiry into the Separation of Aboriginal and Torres Strait Islander Children from their Families states that the placement of children into the protective guardianship of the state involved the state in a fiduciary duty to 'care for, protect and rear' the ward. A fiduciary relationship exists where 'one party is dependent or vulnerable and the other has discretionary powers over the first'.[32] There is a legal responsibility here for the state to use its discretionary powers to care for and protect the children. In effect, though the state took on parental responsibilities and duties in relation to each child, many children were poorly treated after being taken into care by foster families or placed in institutions. The inquiry identified three main breaches of guardianship duties on the part of Protectors and other officials. These were:

- They failed to provide contemporary standards of care to Indigenous children when such standards of care were provided to non-Indigenous children in similar circumstances.
- They failed to protect the children from harm.
- They failed to involve Indigenous parents in decision-making about their children.

All of these breaches in fiduciary duty can be seen to have occurred in the case of children placed into care at Croker Island. Throughout Australia, and notwithstanding the actions of individuals, the standard of institutional care was lower in institutions for Indigenous children than it was in institutions that held non-Indigenous children. The National Inquiry into the Separation of Aboriginal and Torres Strait Islanders from their Families states:

> Many witnesses to the Inquiry spoke of the appalling standards of care in institutions. Former residents told of being cold and hungry, worked too hard but educated too little . . . The mainstream child welfare system was also seriously flawed but children in the mainstream did benefit from advances in knowledge about child development and the effects of institutionalisation many decades before Indigenous children were accorded the same standards of care.[33]

At Croker Island, the conditions were harsh, even by the standards of the time. This is evident in the following description by Lorraine Siwers:

> We didn't have enough food so we had to go looking for bush tucker. We'd get wild apples, berries, cabbage palm, fish, sugarbag [wild honey], lily stems and roots. There was plenty of bush tucker there. They didn't seem to mind that, only if we lost the goats. We were always working in the garden with the goats. One day we were chasing goannas and we lost the goats and they got into the vege garden. We got the biggest flogging and two weeks detention. We had to go to the office. We put on two or three pairs of pants so it wouldn't hurt so much. They gave us a hiding. Electric cords.[34]

A failure to protect these children from harm is apparent. Not only was their physical hurt – as described above – and emotional damage intrinsic to separation from their parents and families, but sexual abuse was also suffered by some children. Keeping these children from their family members placed them at the mercy of institution staff. If they were abused physically, sexually or emotionally they had no one to turn to for protection. The children also suffered through the institutions' failure to provide them with normal affection, such as is experienced in a family. As much as possible, they compensated for this by developing strong emotional bonds among themselves, as is shown in the following description by Lorraine Siwers:

> We are so close now. You can't break off that bond. We look out for each other. We'd make friends with kids from other [Aboriginal] country. But Rita and Eileen and Tommy were special because I knew they were

> from my country. We were all like sisters and brothers, even to this day. We only had each other. We were like one family. The sisters weren't like family. They wouldn't give you a hug at night or tuck you in.[35]

Institutional life aimed to instil in children a work ethic and to prepare them for designated places in the lower echelons of the labour force. At the 1937 Initial Conference of Commonwealth and State Aboriginal Authorities Mr Neville, Commissioner of Native Affairs, Western Australia, stated:

> We say that an idle native is a bad native, and we try to induce them to work one way or another. Even industrial work does not come amiss to the natives. We manufacture about 10,000 garments a year for the natives, and every one of them is manufactured by the natives themselves.[36]

Under the guise of 'domestic training', the girls were required to undertake the tasks needed to keep the institution and its inmates clean and in order. This was not only to gain the work ethic itself, but also because the institutions were at times seriously underfunded, sometimes not even having enough food for the children. Institutional budgets were formulated on the assumption that cleaning and maintenance costs would be minimised by using the labour of the children themselves. Lorraine Siwers recalls:

> We were working like grown-ups, even though we were kids. We went to school and worked after school. We'd play just before tea.[37]

Once the children turned 18, they were free to take their place in the wider community, but even here their actions were guided by institutional policies. One of the primary interests of the administration was that the children not return to the vicinity of their home country, where they would be tempted to renew contact with 'undesirable' relatives. This fear of the supposedly adverse affect of contact between the children and their families is expressed by Mr Harkness, Member of the Aboriginal Protection Board, New South Wales:

> We also have a system of taking girls in the early adolescent stage and training them for domestic service. These girls reach quite a high standard. Unfortunately, of course, if they go back to the old surroundings, they revert to the old habits, and particularly to the lower moral standard, and become the mothers of illegitimate children early in life.[38]

Accordingly, when the time came to leave the institutions the children were encouraged to settle far from their home country. The welfare of the girls received particular attention, arising partly from a vague contemporary respect for women-kind and also, as Brook points out, because the removal of girls served to undermine traditional practices, such as infant betrothal and polygamy, which were abhorred by Europeans Lorraine Siwers recalls:

> None of them wanted us to go to Darwin. They said it was an evil place, 'hell on earth', I think they said. I wish I'd gone back to Darwin. All the good kids were sent interstate and the naughty ones they kept behind for a while and they went to Darwin.[39]

And so the children took up their allotted places in life, trained as a semi-skilled labour forced destined to be subservient to white people. They were equipped for employment in 'suitable' occupations; the boys as stockmen and the girls as domestic servants. It is a grand irony that women such as Lorraine Siwers, stolen to save them from growing up in a 'dirty' environment, ended up cleaning and looking after white children:

Figure 7.2
Lorraine Siwers on the day she left Croker Island for Adelaide, 1958

> I came down [to Adelaide] in 1958. I went to the children's home to work. I was there ten years. I looked after kids, cleaned and cooked. There was a mixture of black and white kids, mainly white, but quite a few from Croker. I got paid £10 a week and found. We used to have to wash everything by hand and then put it in the coppers. We had radio, no TV. We used to listen to 'Blue Hills', 'The Pied Piper' and 'Dad and Dave'. I left when I got married, after nearly ten years. It was my home then. I felt at home because all the kids were still there from Croker. A lot of them went back to find their families and then came back again.[40]

Left: Figure 7.3
Lorraine Siwers,
Adelaide, c. 1983

Below: Figure 7.4
Lorraine Siwers
and her children,
Adelaide, 1983
(from left, Phillip,
Chris, Lorraine,
Debbie and Darren)

The Effects on Family and Community

The forcible removal of their children was devastating to Aboriginal communities. Conceived and implemented as one facet of a policy that systematically disenfranchised Aboriginal people of many of their human rights, it undermined people's dignity and self-esteem. Moreover, it underscored their powerlessness in the face of European laws. They were not even powerful enough to maintain custody of their own children. The findings of the National Inquiry into the Separation of Aboriginal and Torres Strait Islander Children from their Families were:

> The Inquiry was told that the effects damage the children who were forcibly removed, their parents and siblings and their communities. Subsequent generations continue to suffer the effects of parents and grandparents having been forcibly removed, institutionalised, denied contact with their Aboriginality and in some cases traumatised and abused.[41]

A major deficiency in the fiduciary duties of Protectors and other officials was that of failing to involve Indigenous parents in decision-making about their children.[42] Not only were the parents not consulted about the welfare and rearing of their children, but their whereabouts was hidden from them. Lorraine Siwers recalls:

> They didn't tell them where we'd gone. Our family didn't know where they had sent us. Nothing. They couldn't find us. Rita's mum [Daisy Borduk] used to go to that Rita Dixon Home [in Darwin] looking around for us. She just kept going back and forwards to that place, in case there was another lot of kids. She didn't see any of our kids.[43]

The consequences for the families were devastating:

> Later, I asked my sister, 'What did Mum do, afterwards?' She said 'She was always crying, thinking of you. She started getting sick then.' They said she died of a broken heart. My sister said she was never the same after they'd taken me. I swore to God that I'd never let my kids be taken away from me.[44]

Denied the fundamental right to rear their own children, women such as Lorraine's mother became disillusioned and lost confidence in their ability to shape good and meaningful lives. Some took to drink or left their partners, inadvertently providing retrospective 'proof' of the merit of removal policies. The pain and bewilderment caused by these policies is apparent in the meeting between Eileen Cummings and her mother, Flora Lindsay, when Eileen was an adult:

> I said 'Do you know who I am?' Mum said, 'Yes. I've been waiting for you . . . I knew you would come . . . You're my daughter Eileen, who they took away from me. Them white people just took you away . . . I worked hard all my life. I wasn't a bad woman. I wasn't a bad mother.

> I don't know why they had to take you away. I could have looked after you.' All the time she had tears silently pouring down her face.[45]

This conversation reveals the unresolved grief and self-questioning felt by the mothers. It is easy to imagine Florrie turning the problem over in her mind, looking for reassurance that it wasn't her fault, that there wasn't something that she could have done to prevent it. Her words also reveal a sense of betrayal. She'd followed the rules. She's worked hard. She wasn't a bad woman. And still they took her daughter away. It didn't make sense that one thing could follow from the other. Eileen's feelings on this matter are eloquent:

> Their rights were removed from them but at the same time they didn't know how to work with the pain or how to cope with it. Mum wouldn't talk about it. She wouldn't even talk about my father. She just said, 'He's gone now. He's a white man. He rode around all the time on horses.' Mum's husband Chuckerduck, that's the man I really call my father.[46]

The inability of Aboriginal mothers to talk about the removal of their children is eloquent testimony in itself. As well, one way in which Aboriginal people deal with an overwhelming problem is to 'make it small', rather than 'talking it out' as Europeans tend to do. This incapacity to discuss the children's removal was common throughout Australia, as is evident in the submission by Link-Up, a New South Wales organisation that reunites separated children and their families, to the National Inquiry:

> In preparing this submission we found that Aboriginal women were unwilling and unable to speak about the immense pain, grief and anguish that losing their children had caused them. That point was so strong that we were unable to find a mother that had healed enough to be able to speak, and to share her experiences with us and the Commission.[47]

The effects on family and community were particularly extensive, given that parenting and nurturing are widely shared in Indigenous societies. Each child was embedded in a network of kinship relationships and each removal had an impact upon a range of family members, depriving them of their role as it applied to that child, and of their dreams and ambitions for that role. Siblings were denied a playmate; aunts were denied the right to be mother-equivalent;

Figure 7.5
Daisy Borduk and Lorraine Siwers, Barunga, 1988

uncles were denied the right to pass on traditional and ceremonial knowledge; grandparents were denied a grandchild to look after them in their old age – with the removal of each child, all of the roles and attendant dreams woven around that child became void.

Moreover, the removal of children instilled a sense of shame in the community as a whole. Partly, this was to do with their incapacity to protect the child but there was also a fear that the children would adopt white values and reject their Aboriginal heritage once they had grown up. Jimmy Wessan, an elder of Wugularr community, comments:

> From the start, even before I been born, they send them yellowfella kids other places, la mununga [white people] way. We couldn't stop them [taking the children]. We couldn't stop them. [When they were gone] we thought about them kids, but after a long while we only thought about them a little bit. We didn't like to think about them. We can't do nothing about it. Just leave it. When they were big we thought 'Might be they mununga [white people] now. Might be they don't want to know blackfella.'[48]

When they were adults, many of these children found their way back to their communities but few were in a position to take up what would have been their 'normal' role in their home communities. Most maintain contact, but live in other places. Those that did stay on are a source of pride to their families, as is evident in this discussion with Roy Anderson:

> The government took my sister [Alma Cadell] away when I was ten years old. At Eva Valley. We were staying in the bush, you know, come in for a feed and then go back bush. Then I had to go to school at Barunga.

When she was taken away she was staying at the Rita Dixon school. She found a boyfriend, got married and got a lot of kids. Then she came back when she had kids. She had to look around for her mother and father and all her family.

That's my sister's house [pointing]. My sister is staying in town for a while, but she'll be back. That's her little son, standing there. Another boy [is] working at Nitmiluk. Another girl, she's in Darwin. Sometimes she [my sister] stays here a long time and sometimes she stays in town.[49]

New Warriors and Nurturers

Throughout Australia, the effects of forcible removal were wide-ranging and devastating, continuing on into the adult lives of the children, their families and their communities. The need to provide these children with monetary compensation was recognised in Recommendation 14 of the National Inquiry into the Separation of Aboriginal and Torres Strait Islander Children from their Families. This suggested that compensation be provided under the following categories:[50]

- Racial discrimination.
- Arbitrary deprivation of liberty.
- Pain and suffering.
- Abuse, including physical, sexual and emotional abuse.
- Disruption of family life.
- Loss of cultural rights and fulfilment.
- Loss of native title rights.
- Labour exploitation.
- Economic loss.
- Loss of opportunities.

Every child that was stolen suffered from all, or most of, the above. In particular, separation from their families and cultural heritage had profound effects on the children's abilities as adults to function within Aboriginal communities. Denied education in Aboriginal languages, culture and traditional responsibilities, these children were not equipped to take their normal place in Aboriginal societies. The National Inquiry into the Separation of Aboriginal and Torres Strait Islander Children from their Families found that:[51]

The complete separation of the children from any connection, communication or knowledge about their Indigenous heritage has had

> profound effects on their experience of Aboriginality and their participation in the Aboriginal community as adults.

Jimmy Wesan expresses the loss from the point of view of both the children and the community:

> If they stay they would know everything now, law side, ceremony side, but they didn't learn anything. They only follow that one law, that mununga [whitefella] law now, instead of that blackfella law. They lost. They been lost.[52]

The Stolen Generations did not grow up to be 'the same' as white Australians. They grew up to be Indigenous people who acquired the same skills as white Australians. Though they took their allotted places in the social order during those first years in the wider community, as the years passed many of them shaped individual niches that integrated their Aboriginal identities and the need to be part of their own communities. As adults, they were faced with the job of rescuing their Aboriginality and shaping a place for themselves in their home communities. Some found themselves unequal to the task, clinging to the identities manufactured for them in institutions and foster homes.[53] Others used the skills they had gained from a Western education to work for their communities and advance the struggle of Aboriginal people. One unanticipated outcome of removal practices was that the government had actually constructed a new grouping of Indigenous Australians. Paradoxically, the practices that had been employed to assuage the fear that children of mixed descent would become leaders in acts of resistance had actually produced a new class of warriors and nurturers.

These warriors and nurturers used their European education and skills to work for their communities and advance the struggle of Aboriginal people. This can be seen in the contemporary lives of Eileen Cummings, Rita Tingey and Lorraine Siwers. Eileen, for example, left the mission at 15 years of age and was placed in a foster home in Darwin until she was 18. She continued her education in Brisbane and was the first qualified Aboriginal teacher in the Northern Territory. Later she became a Policy and Liaison Officer in the Office of Women's Policy, Department of Chief Minister, Northern Territory, providing policy advice to the Chief Minister on matters pertaining to the status of women. Eileen was fully responsible for co-ordinating the consultations to facilitate the

Figure 7.6
Aboriginal delegation to the 4th World Archaeological Congress, Cape Town, South Africa, 1999.
Back row: (from left) Eileen Cummings, Peter Manabaru, Irene Fisher, Jimmy Wesan.
Front row: (from left) Ken Isaacson, Richard Hunter. Photo: C.Smith

development of the Aboriginal Family Violence Strategy and is the co-author of this Strategy. She was also the Program Manager of the Aboriginal Family Violence Program when it was launched in 1995. For many years she has been on committees, boards and councils at international, national and local levels addressing Indigenous issues.

Today, the children of the Stolen Generations connect with country in a variety of ways, some of which may not be apparent to a passing eye. For example, Rita Tigney's work with Indigenous plants has an element of returning to country:

> I work with Greening Australia, working in the bush tucker area, the Aboriginal Land Care Education Programme. I learnt a lot from my mother's mob, from Auntie Margaret Katherine. I've been working there about seven or eight years.
>
> I work with Aboriginal communities, helping with land-care and nurseries. Either growing them [the plants] here, or acting as a nursery for their country. We collect the seeds, get them growing and take

> them back to their country. Sometimes I take seeds back to Croker Island . . . [That is okay with local Aboriginal people] because they know who we are. The bush tucker at Croker is different from here.[53]

In this way, Rita maintains her links with both her mother's country and also the country in which she grew up.

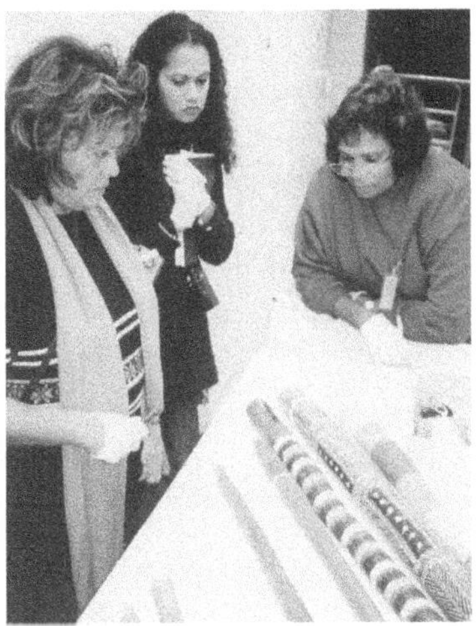

Left: Figure 7.7
Eileen Cummings, Irene Fisher and Tara Dodd examining Indigenous Australian collections at the National Museum of Natural History, Smithsonian Institution, Washington, DC, 1999

Right: Figure 7.8
Rita Tingey working with Darwin Garden Club

Others, such as Lorraine Siwers, have shaped their life niches to provide long-distance support for their home communities. Based in Adelaide and 3,000 kilometres from the Barunga–Wugularr region, Lorraine has regular contact with community members when they go south for hospitalisation, a regular occurrence in Aboriginal communities. Her commitment is vital to the well being of community members when they are sick and most vulnerable. Along with Rita, Lorraine has looked after Rita Tingey's mother, Daisy Borduk, when she was in hospital in Adelaide. Lorraine comments:

Mostly my family come to visit. My immediate family. My sister's children and their children and some people that I grew up with on Croker Island, we still keep in touch. People come down to hospital and they come and stay with me. I've got a friend at the Royal Adelaide Hospital and she let me know if someone from the community comes down. They stay with me overnight, or sometimes for a couple of days. Sometimes they feel lost, coming to the city. It seems strange to them coming to the big city, especially if they haven't been here before. It's good for them to have someone from the same country looking after them. I can understand them. Sometimes it's a bit hard for white people to understand what they are saying.

It benefits me as well as them. I just like to be with my people. Since I've found them, I'd like to have a relationship with them as much as I can. I think it is because it's what I missed out as a small child.[54]

Eight

Growing Empowerment

There remains a determination among many communities, both Aboriginal and non-Aboriginal, to obtain a greater degree of control in respect of matters over which they have the greatest knowledge and in respect of which they have the most acute and intimate concern.

James Robertson, the Minister for Community Development, Jim Robertson, introducing the notion of community self-government to the Legislative Assembly of the Northern Territory.[1]

The recent history of Aboriginal Australians has been one of growing empowerment. However, this has not come easily or at a small cost. Some initiatives, such as land rights and outstations, combined to revitalise traditional Aboriginal power structures and political traditions. Others programmes and schemes were less successful, constrained by inadequate funding, insufficient or inappropriate training and a continuing inability of European administrators and government officials to allow Aboriginal people to take control of their own destinies. However, despite the dead-ends and disappointments, the last few decades have seen important advances in the empowerment of Aboriginal Australians.

Legislative Emancipation

The major legislative restrictions discriminating against Aboriginal people on the basis of race were erased from the legislation of Australian States and Territories during 1964. The passage in the Northern Territory of the Social Welfare Ordinance 1964 coincided with the repealing of the Welfare Ordinance 1953 and around this time there were many other racially based ordinances amended in order to omit specific reference to Aboriginals. These included the Firearms Ordinance, Licensing Ordinance, Poisons Ordinance, Dangerous Drugs Ordinance, Methylated Spirits Ordinance, Intestate Wards Ordinance, Native Constabulary Ordinance and Registration of Dogs Ordinance. All of these Ordinances were racially based and aimed at controlling specific aspects of Aboriginal peoples' behaviour. The manner in which this legislative emancipation was presented to the Australian public is remarkable for the lack of critical analysis of the situation which preceded it. This is exemplified in an item in *Australia Through Time*:

> NT ABORIGINES NOW FULL CITIZENS
> Thursday, 20 February, 1964
>
> Aborigines in the Northern Territory are now full citizens after legislation passed through the NT's Legislative Council today. The Social Welfare Act brings the Territory's Aboriginal population onto equal footing with whites, after some had received partial political and other rights in recent years.
>
> The amendments abolish the legal concept of wardship, applicable since 1953, which gave the Territory administration formal responsibility and control over most of the Territory's Aboriginal people.
>
> The Act provides for the continuation of Aboriginal reserves to prevent the exploitation of the indigenous inhabitants of the Northern Territory. It also allows Aborigines to own and trade property and cohabit with non-Aborigines.

The granting of citizenship set the ground for the most important transition in Indigenous affairs in thirty years, the movement away from assimilation towards Indigenous self-management and, finally, self-determination. An early step on this path was the granting of enfranchisement. In the Northern Territory this occurred in 1962. It was not until 1967, however, that Indigenous people were included in Australian census counts. This was in response to a referendum held in May, 1967 at which almost 92 per cent of Australians voted to make the necessary amendment to the Federal constitution.[2] For the first time, Aboriginal people were reckoned among the Australian population and ascribed equal rights under the law. The adoption of these constitutional changes was a prerequisite for the major policy changes that would occur in Aboriginal affairs over subsequent decades.

At that time Aboriginal people in the Barunga were only beginning to develop a wider political consciousness. For them, the impact of the legislative changes were felt in small things, such as the right to buy a beer. Peter Manabaru was travelling in Arnhem Land with the anthropologist Ken Maddock when the news came through:

> That many people been travelling longa that Ken Maddock. All the Dalabon [Ngalkbon] people been go with him to that Dalabon country. We been listening to that radio, wireless radio. [Ken Maddock said] 'Oh, that citizen open now. When you go back, you mob can have beer now'. We didn't believe him, but when we came back, it really one, now. It been open everywhere.[3]

Despite these landmark reforms in the legislative positioning of Indigenous Australians, assimilation polices in the Northern Territory remained essentially unchallenged until the 1970s. The impetus for radical change came at the Federal level with the 1972 election of a Labor Government. This government created a Commonwealth Department of Aboriginal Affairs and in 1974 the Minister for Aboriginal Affairs, Jim Cavenagh, summarised Departmental policy as one which sought to 'make equality a reality for Aboriginal Australians' through acting 'in the closest consultation with Aboriginal communities and individuals'.[4] During this period, the focus changed from the care and protection of Aboriginal peoples to acceptance of their right to manage their own affairs. A fundamental difference between this and earlier periods is that policies were based upon the premise that Aboriginal and non-Aboriginal people were equals, though different, so it followed that the new policies had to be based upon recognition of the rights and abilities of Aboriginal peoples to determine their own futures.

Aboriginal land rights became a critical component of self-determination, supported at a federal level by both labour and liberal governments. In 1972 the federal Labour Government established The Aboriginal Land Rights Commission, whose charter was to examine and make recommendations on the manner in which Aboriginal rights to land might be implemented in the Northern Territory.[5] In 1974 the Commission presented its final report to the Governor-General, Sir Paul Hasluck and a little later, the *Aboriginal Land Rights (Northern Territory) Act* 1976 was passed in the Federal Parliament. The enactment of this legislation meant that Aboriginal reserves, such as those at Bamyili and Beswick Station, reverted to Aboriginal ownership. After so long under the juristriction of European administrators, Aboriginal relished the idea of looking after themselves:

> Jawoyn take over land council ourselves. This our land. Jawoyn got to make it their own self. Our land. We got to look after ourselves.[6]

The *Aboriginal Land Rights Act* remains the most significant such legislation in Australia. Under this legislation about half of the Northern Territory was returned to traditional ownership.

Community Self-Management

The recent history of settlements in the Barunga–Wugularr region is one in which Aboriginal people have obtained greater, but never absolute, control over their daily lives. The Aboriginalisation of community management is reflected in changes in the names of settlements. In 1984 the Bamyili Town Council changed the name of the Bamyili community to Barunga, the traditional Jawoyn name for the area. In the same year Eva Valley Station was bought at auction on behalf of local Aboriginal people by the Aboriginal Development Corporation, with funds supplied by the Aboriginal Benefit Trust Account.[7] The name of the station was changed to Manyallaluk. Two years later the Beswick community was renamed Wugularr.

During this period the Northern Territory government pushed the idea of community self-government. This concept underpinned the *Local Government Act* of 1985, which came into effect in July 1986. Under the provisions of this Act a number of Aboriginal communities, including those of Barunga and Wugularr, were in a position to choose to administer local government functions themselves, for the first time gaining control over the management of their daily lives.

On 16th October 1986 the Barunga and Beswick town councils were replaced by the Barunga–Wugularr Community Government Council which became an incorporated body under the *Local Government Act*, 1985. These schemes are used with the flexibility that is characteristic of all Aboriginal political structures and changes in alliances between the three communities in the region are evident in changes in their incorporation status. On 1st July 1993, the Barunga–Wugularr Community Government Scheme was replaced by the Barunga–Manyallaluk Community Government Scheme and the Wugularr Community Government Scheme.

Despite the rhetoric of self-management, the primary role of community government councils is to perform the normal administrative functions of European municipality. The functions of Barunga–Manyallaluk Community Government Council are written in accord with European, not Aboriginal, conceptions of work, property and social order. They include:

- The establishment and maintenance of parks, gardens and recreational areas.
- The establishment and maintenance of sporting facilities, libraries, public toilets and ablution blocks, community halls and so forth.
- The provision of services for the collection and disposal of garbage.
- The collection of electricity, water and sewerage charges.
- The provision of adult education and vocational and other training.
- The management of community employment programmes.
- The promotion and provision of community welfare, health, and care facilities.
- The control or prohibition of animals.
- The development and maintenance of roads within the community government area and, for reward, the development and maintenance of roads outside the community government area.
- The establishment and operation of pastoral and commercial enterprises.
- The provision and maintenance of cemeteries.
- The promotion and development of tourist attractions, the provision and maintenance of tourist facilities, the production and selling of artefacts and souvenirs and the management and control of sites of historic interest.
- The support and encouragement of artistic, cultural and sporting activities.

Recognition of the rights of both land owners and the people who live there all their lives are implicit in the structure of both community government schemes. The major language groups living at Barunga and Eva Valley are formally empowered in a provision of the Barunga–Manyallaluk Community Government Scheme that the council shall consist of fourteen members and 'shall include two persons from and to represent each of the Jawoyn, Mangarrai, Mara, Myilly, Ngarrbun and Rembarrnga language groups and two persons from and to represent electors who are not members of any of these six language groups'. This is in contrast to the Wugularr Community Government Scheme, which concentrates power in the hands of Jawoyn people. This scheme provides for a council of nine members which 'shall include four persons from the Jawoyn language group and one person from each of the Mangarrai, Mara, Myilly, Rembarrnga and Ritharrngu language groups'. In both cases the President and Vice-President are elected from among themselves by the members of the council and may derive from any language group. The need to have greater representation of Jawoyn people on the Wugularr Council could be in response to the very low numbers of Jawoyn people living in that community (only seven in 1999, see Chapter Nine). In contrast, Barunga has a significant Jawoyn population, including the senior traditional owner for the region, Phyllis Wiynjorroc, and her family.

Consistent with Aboriginal power structures, the control of council operations has always been in the hands of a relatively few families. Aboriginal members of the permanent staff at Barunga in 1984 included three Ngalkbon people: Leo Lee, as Town Clerk; Cyril McCartney, as President; and Lorraine Bennett, assistant in the Commonwealth Employment Service Office. Administrative duties were undertaken by Sybil Ranch, the Jawoyn granddaughter of Phyllis Wiynjorroc. By the early 1990s little appeared to have changed. In 1991 and 1992 Cyril McCartney was still President of the Council and Robert Lee, the son of Daisy Borduk, had taken over the position of Town Clerk when his older brother Leo died in the late 1980s. Assisted by various members of her family, Sybil Ranch continued to conduct administrative work in the council office during 1990s and early 2000s. A Ngalkbon man Geoffrey Wallah had a short stint as President during the mid 1990s but was replaced by Nell Brown, the daughter of Phyllis Wiynjorroc, and in the late 1990s Anthony Lee, the younger brother of Robert Lee, became Council President.

A major variation to this pattern occurred during 1993 when Jeffrey McDonald was voted Council President. Jeffrey McDonald's election was significant in three main respects. First, it was an important structural change, since most of the previous council presidents, including the long-term presidents Ray Fordimail and Cyril McCartney, had been of the Ngalkbon language group. Jeffrey was the senior Jawoyn man in the region, though he was not of the Bugula clan and hence a traditonal owner of Barunga in the same sense as Phyllis Wiynjorroc. Second, it moved power squarely from younger men back into the hands of a senior man. Third, and perhaps most important, it gave the lie to the fallacy that a council president needed to be literate – while Jeffrey McDonald spoke excellent English he could neither read nor write. Nevertheless, he was knowledgeable about both Aboriginal and non-Aboriginal political and social issues, partly through being a long-term member of the executive of the Jawoyn Association, and he performed his council duties with great competency, assisted by the staff and his young wife Ida.

One of the main functions of community councils in the Barunga–Wugularr region is to administer Community Employment Development Programmes (CDEP) which are the major source of employment in these communities. The CDEP scheme was piloted at the Barunga community in 1977. By 1993–94 it involved 279 communities across the nation, and a total of 28,000 participants.[8] Under this scheme, unemployed Aboriginals and Torres Strait Islanders are paid the equivalent of the unemployment benefit in return for work undertaken for community organisations. In proportion to the income generated, the work is generally part-time. However, the work involved in the CDEP scheme is usually menial. In the Barunga–Wugularr region it includes the maintenance of parks, gardens and other community amenities, the collection of garbage and provision of other municipal services, as well as the production of artefacts for sale.

In recent years there has been serious critique of the CDEP scheme.[9] One recurring criticism is that it is structured by non-Aboriginal notions of work. For example, people in their sixties are excluded from the scheme, even though they are traditionally the main people to produce artefacts. This seems to be based on the European notion that older people should be retired rather than working, combined with a recognition that older people can obtain a comparable income through the pension. Similarly, few women are included in the scheme, again in part because women of working age usually have children and an alternative source of government income. One of the most serious problems with the CDEP scheme, however, is that it has allowed governments to avoid fulfilling their normal municipal responsibilities since the scheme gives them access to 'free' labour. In this way, the CDEP scheme acts to inhibit normal employment opportunities. In those cases where communities are self-managed Aboriginal people become complicit in this constraining of job opportunities and the resulting high level of under-employment. In fact, Berndardi goes so far as to characterise the CDEP scheme as a form of 'welfare colonialism' in which Aboriginal people have been positioned so that they subject themselves.[10]

The CDEP scheme is just one facet of community self-government, but it illustrates the manner in which self-government is constrained by the state and shaped by European concepts and values. Writing in 1986, Malcolm Mowbray addressed this issue:

> Direct repression of the Aboriginal interests at the local level is no longer politically acceptable. State control needs to be disguised, hence the great virtue of community government with its democratic image. The myth of community control also helps make it possible to 'blame the victims' for service deficiencies. The community government provisions of the Local Government Act appear most progressive and flexible, especially in contrast to most other local government legislation. However, the freedom this gives for self-determination of local schemes is thwarted by overarching ministerial and departmental control . . . The major channel for government control, however, is not in the legislation itself, but in the financial arrangements that determine the scope and impact of council activities. These involve both the absolute amount of funds transferred as well as the extent to which they are tied to specific uses.[11]

The Outstation Movement

The 'outstation' or 'homelands' movement, in which people return to live on their clan lands, arose during the 1970s and 1980s. It became a major way through which Aboriginal people were able to reclaim traditional lands. Outstations usually have two or three houses, which are lived in by different groupings of extended families, with a core population of around ten to fifteen people. The outstations used by Aboriginal people in the Barunga–Wugularr region are located in central Arnhem Land, within a relatively easy drive from the township of Gulin Gulin (Bulman). The main outstations that are important to Barunga people are Weemol, Momob, Gulpulyu and Blue Water (Morboarrn).

The outstation movement empowers Aboriginal people in a numbers of ways. Firstly, it gives people the authority of living on their own lands again, not in a settlement that is on somebody else's lands. This is an important difference to Aboriginal people, comparable to the European distinction between renting and owning a house. The second way in which outstations are empowering is that

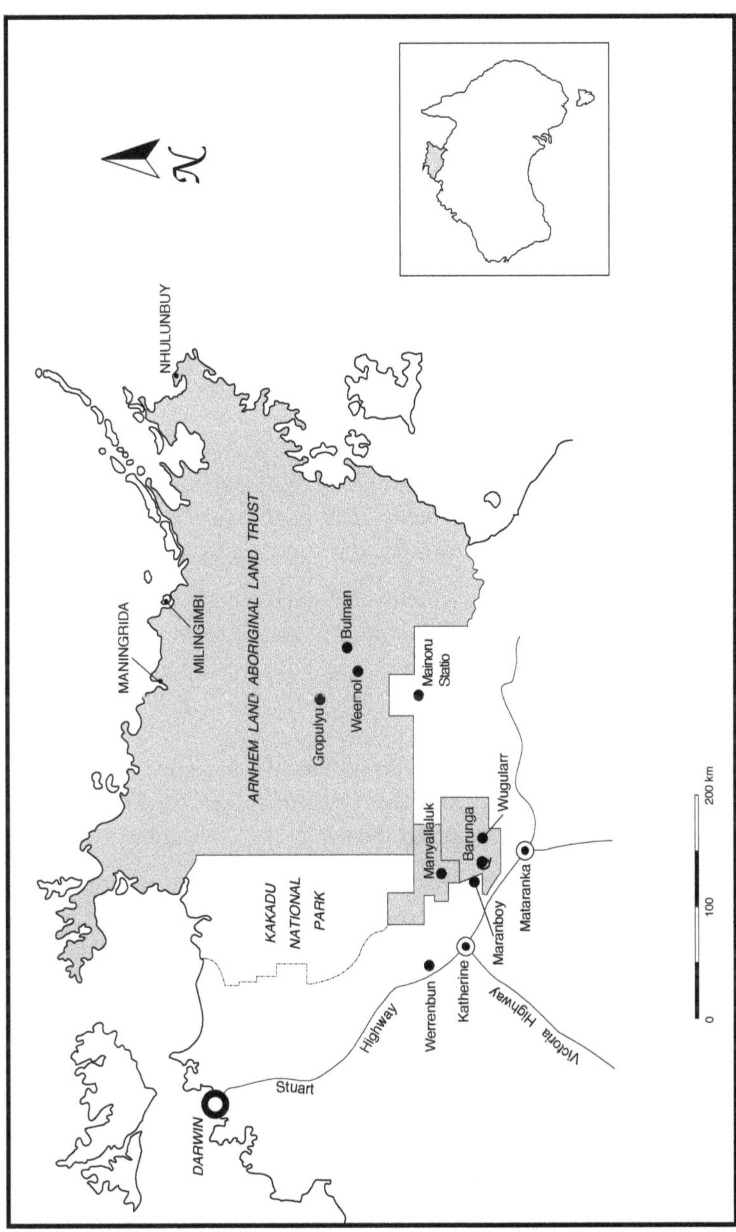

Map 8.1
Location of community settlements and outstations in the Barunga–Wugularr region

they are a place of refuge for troubled members of the extended family. Thus, young boys who have been in difficulties or men who are giving up drinking are likely to go to live on an outstation for a period of time. Outstations are away from the temptations and stresses of the bigger settlements and provide the opportunity for a quiet lifestyle, with the chance to pursue traditional pursuits such as fishing and hunting. People living on outstations often make artefacts, as well, the very act of which reinforces the value of Aboriginal cultural practices. Outstations are places in which people are able to develop their own mix of traditional and introduced economic pursuits and where they are away from the intervention of non-Aboriginal people in their daily lives. They are places of independence, power and cultural renewal.

The construction of an outstation is a statement of affiliation to country and either prompts or builds on a decision to go 'Mummy-way' or 'Daddy-way'. This is evident in the decisions made by Steven (Patrick) Willika, the son of Lilly Willika:

> When I go back to Dad's country, I'm more at home. When I go back to Mum's country, I'm a little bit at home, but not so comfortable. I keep quiet down there [like a visitor], but I feel at home here. And I feel comfortable speaking with Gagadu and Mielli people. Aboriginal people don't want to talk for another's country.
>
> So now we are building an outstation. We can stay there. We can sit down there forever. Bush tucker everywhere. Teach the kids culture, so they can get strong and stay there.

In rare cases outstations have developed into small communities. For example, Weemol, located only six kilometres from Gulin Gulin,

Figure 8.1 Ryan Baruwei talking with Gary Jackson, Werrenbun outstation, 2003

has developed into a community of around 100 people, most of whom are Ngalkbon, whereas mostly Rembarrnga people live at Gulin Gulin. As with many outstations in this region, the houses at Weemol often are made from local materials, such as stone, and are designed in consultation with the Aboriginal occupants. The result is sturdy houses with enclosed sleeping areas and open living areas. These houses are used in a practical manner, without the emotional investment placed in them by Europeans. Cowlishaw addresses this issue in terms of Bulman housing, but her comments are equally applicable to houses throughout the Barunga–Wugularr region:

Figure 8.2
Maggie Tacumba weaving a basket at Weemol outstation, 1991

> At Bulman, houses are treated functionally and flexibly, with no great pride invested in the ownership of the building and less on maintaining an ordered aesthetics. They are still being tried out. Practices in relation to houses have not become weighty responsibilities demanding elaborate and endlessly repeated housekeeping rituals and maintenance.[12]

The outstation movement is significant because it developed as an Aboriginal solution to the problems of larger communities, in which people live in much closer proximity to each other than they did traditionally. It countered a tendency with government policy to make the settlement, rather than the people, the focus of administration. This movement towards decentralisation originally caught Australian government officials by surprise. Once he had come to terms with Aboriginal aspirations in this are, the eminent economist H.C. Coombs provided key support to the outstation movement and he promoted decentralisation as one of the key tenets of Aboriginal self-determination.[13]

The Problem with Self-Determination

The notion of self-determination gained momentum during the 1970s and 1980s, based on the hope that the 'Aboriginal problem' would be solved if Aboriginals were to take control of their own destinies. This radical new policy was advanced by the triumvirate of Nugget Coombs, the anthropologist W.H. Stanner and the senior public servant Barry Dexter. It produced a number of important reform projects but has stopped short of success in terms of the promotion of Aboriginal agendas. Though the two are often linked, self-determination is different to community self-management. Self-management involves the administration of government programmes and local government functions as well as the management of enterprises on behalf of Aboriginal communities. Self-determination, however, is predicated on the notion that Aboriginal people should be able to shape policies that will affect their people; that Aboriginal people should have a major role in planning their own futures. These changes in attitude are expressed by the Royal Commission into Aboriginal Deaths in Custody:

> Non-Aboriginal people must face the fact that for a very long time we have proceeded on the basis that Aboriginal people were inferior, were unable to make decisions affecting themselves, that we knew what was best for them ... This is true both for public officials and for private persons. It is an attitude which is very deeply resented by Aboriginal people, and would indeed be by us if roles were reversed ... it is important that non-Aboriginal people not try and impose on Aboriginal people their non-Aboriginal ideas of what is good, wise or moral but to let Aboriginal people feel their own way ... the whole thrust of this report is directed towards empowerment of Aboriginal society on the basis of their deeply held desire, their demonstrated capacity, their democratic right to exercise, according to circumstances, maximum control over their own lives and that of their communities.

Today, it is clear that self-determination has worked only to a limited extent. This is because Aboriginal people have not been given freedom to develop and pursue their own visions. The visions and projects that have been supported have always been those that keyed most closely into European ideas of social and economic progress. In the Barunga–Wugularr region, this has resulted in funding for projects that were never going to work according to a European pattern. Some projects failed simply because they were never going to work. Others were adapted to suit Aboriginal kinship and social systems, such as the creche which is used in a vague kind of rotation by family groups with young children, including mothers and grandmothers, rather than on the European model of paid carers looking after a group of children to which they are not related.

The problem with self-determination is that, like assimilation, it demands major and not always welcome adaptations by Aboriginal people.[14] The idea is laudable but it has not been realised in practice. Self-determination is geared towards producing outcomes that are consonant with the goals and aspirations of Europeans, rather than those of Aboriginal people. It is aimed at the effective management of communities, the establishment of viable economic enterprises and, finally, obtaining the material achievements and attendant lifestyles that are such an integral component of European value systems. This is not to say that Aboriginal people do not want material goods, but rather that self-determination has been structured by material, rather than spiritual or religious values. While there is much funding for economic development, in terms of need there is still a dearth of funding for the development of projects which arise from and reinforce Aboriginal cultural values. Frustration with self-determination is expressed succinctly by a non-Aboriginal educator from Yuendumu, Wendy Baada:

> We are face to face with a really, free spontaneous people, and all we can think of is shoving our repressive, materialistic 'hung-up' culture down their throats as fast as we can. And we think they're very *backward* because they aren't picking it up quickly. I don't believe in the new 'self-determination' thing. It isn't. It's just another step in the same plan – to push the yapa [Warlpiri people] into running our kind of town in our way.[15]

While Baada's views are a little pessimistic there is no doubt that self-determination has a long way to go if it's to be successful. Most importantly, it needs to be structured so that it leaves room for the emergence and development of Aboriginal ideas that are *not* consonant with those of a European mind-set.

Nine

Surviving the Present

They [Aboriginal people] probably have the highest growth rate, the highest birth rate, the highest death rate, the worst health and housing and the lowest educational, occupational, economic, social and legal status of any identifiable section of the Australian population.

The first report of the National Population Inquiry[1]

The world inhabited by Indigenous Australians at the start of the third millennium is dramatically different to that inhabited by other Australians. The Indigenous world is a place of astonishingly high unemployment and depressingly low incomes, it is a world in which Indigenous people have a life expectancy around 20 years less than their non-Indigenous counterparts; a world in which they are admitted to hospital three times more often than other Australians and their babies are three times more likely to die before the age of five than non-Indigenous babies. It is a world in which two laws operate and in which Indigenous people disproportionately find themselves incarcerated in Australian gaols. There are serious problems to do with alcohol and substance abuse in this world and the rates of youth suicide are at an all-time high. In the contemporary Indigenous world it is an act of tenacity and courage just to survive.

In such a situation, one might expect Indigenous people simply to give up – to leave their lands en masse in search of jobs in the cities, and to forget their extended families once they had achieved a decent income for themselves. One might also expect them to forget their traditional lands as they moved to more affluent areas of the country, but this hasn't happened. Indigenous people still sustain and nurture the core parts of their identities. The ancestral past still plays a role in shaping the present. The bonds between family and kin are as strong as ever. The hereditary ties to the land are unbroken. And the importance placed on living an Indigenous, rather then a European, life is undiminished.

The history of contact has shown that Indigenous people are survivors. They are resourceful, resilient and adaptive. In the contemporary world, the question that arises is how can they best control their survival, given the constraints of the circumstances into which they are born. What strategies and strengths do Indigenous people draw upon to balance the challenges of contemporary life with the necessity of maintaining their culture and identities? And how?

A Growing Population

Indigenous populations have the highest growth rate of any sector of the Australian population, and censuses have shown a dramatic increase in recent years. At the end of June 1996 around 2.1 per cent of the total population of Australia identified itself as being of Indigenous origin.[2] This showed an increase of 33 per cent in the Indigenous population (from 265,371 to 352,970) since the previous census of 1991, which itself showed an increase of 16 per cent over the census of 1986.[3] The annual growth rate in the Indigenous population was 2.3 per cent, significantly higher than the rate for the total population of 1.2 per cent.[4] This growth rate can be attributed to a higher birth rate as well as an increase in self-identification by people of Aboriginal and Torres Strait Islander descent.

The 1996 Census of Population and Housing conducted by the Australian Bureau of Statistics showed that the age profile of the Indigenous Australian population was different from that of the majority, with a higher proportion of people under the age of 15 years and a lower proportion over the age of 65. Around 40 per cent of the Indigenous population was under 15 years old, in comparison to 21 per cent for the population as a whole. By contrast, only 2.6 per cent of the Indigenous population was over 65 years, in comparison to 12.0 per cent for the total population. At 30th June 1996 the Indigenous population had a median age of 20.1 years, much younger than the median 34.0 for the total population.[5]

These national trends are consistent with specific figures recently collected from the Wugularr community. At 1st November 1999 there were 451 people living at Wugularr. Of these, 198 (44 per cent of the community) were under 18 years old. In contrast, only

2.9 per cent was older than 65 years and only 12.7 per cent 41 years or older. These data show a growing community, one that is numerically dominated by young people and with a sparse representation of older people.

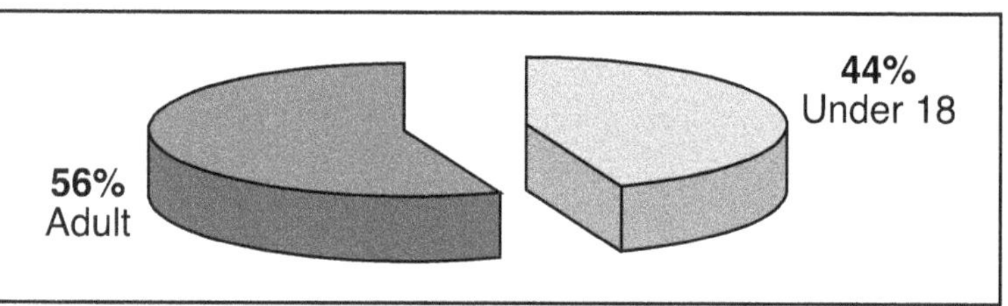

Figure 9.1
Ratio of Young People to Adults, Wugularr Community, 1999

The age profile for the Wugularr community shows how few old people are living there. Only 13 people are over 60 years of age – only 2.6 per cent, highlighting what a rare resource old people are for the community as a whole. This is especially so for Aboriginal societies, such as those at Barunga and Wugularr, in which old people are the repositories of cultural information and knowledge.

These figures demonstrate much more than a high level of fertility in Indigenous populations. They reflect the limited employment

Figure 9.2
Young members of Phyllis Wiynjorroc's family, Barunga, 1998

options available to young women, as well as the continued importance of family and kin. It is not until they have children that young women at Barunga and Wugularr usually are considered to be truly adult. The age profile data also indicate high levels of mortality, which are related to the harsh economic circumstances and the abysmal health and living conditions of many Indigenous groups. All this aside, the data give the lie to any argument that Indigenous populations are 'dying out'. Throughout Australia Aboriginal populations are growing, not only numerically but also as a percentage of the total population.

Income and Employment

The average income of Indigenous peoples is much lower than that of other Australians. As at August 1996, the median weekly personal income of Aboriginal and Torres Strait Islanders was $218 nationwide – considerably below the $294, the median weekly personal income recorded for the population as a whole.[6] The discrepancy was greatest in the Northern Territory, where the figure was $185, reflecting a disparity of $109 (or around 59 per cent) per week. These figures reflect the very high levels of unemployment or under-employment in Indigenous communities. At 30 June 1996, the unemployment rate among Aboriginal people was 22.7 per cent, about 2.5 times the national average of 9.2 per cent. However, even when Aboriginal people were able to find employment, their income was likely to be substantially below that of non-Aboriginal people. At $366 compared to $492, the median weekly personal income for employed Indigenous people was 25.6 per cent lower than that recorded for the total population.

These national trends are apparent in the situation within the Barunga–Wugularr region. At 1st November 1999, 48.2 per cent of the Wugularr community was of an age suitable for employment, that is, between 18 and 60 years.[7] Only 16 (i.e. 7.3 per cent) of these 218 people had full-time employment. These people were employed in community service positions at the council, the school, the shop and the clinic. These data show a combined under-employment/unemployment rate of 92.7 per cent. These figures are not extraordinary for Indigenous Australian communities in rural areas, but they are masked by the Community Development Employment Programme (CDEP), a work-for-the-dole scheme designed specifically for Aboriginal communities. At

1st November 1999 the Wugularr Council had 128 places on this scheme, which provides 'employment' in a range of positions relating to community development, such as maintaining the school grounds and the production of artefacts. This is overwhelmingly in a part-time capacity, netting people an income that is the equivalent of unemployment benefits. However, even if CDEP is counted as 'employment', the unemployment rate among Indigenous people is disturbing. In 1991 the unemployment rate among Aboriginal people nation-wide was 30.8 per cent – 2.7 times the national average.[8]

All this results in low levels of income, not only for individuals, but for Indigenous communities as a whole. The 1996 Australian Bureau of Statistics (ABS) estimates that for the Northern Territory the average annual income in Indigenous communities is around $9,620, consistent with the situation in both the Barunga and Wugularr communities and the major factor in the economic disadvantage suffered by Indigenous people.

A solution sometimes put forward proposes that Indigenous people should move to the cities, where more work can be found; that they should become a more mobile workforce, like contemporary non-Indigenous populations. However, this is not a viable solution for many Indigenous peoples. Ties to their traditional lands and to their families who are living on those lands pull them back to their own country. Figures from the ABS demonstrate the strength of this continuity in Indigenous people's relationships to traditional lands. In 1996 approximately 32 per cent of Aboriginal and Torres Strait Islander peoples lived in rural or remote areas, compared with just under 15 per cent of all Australians. Apart from this, Indigenous ties to land and kin are not bonds that Australians should be seeking to loosen, since they exist at the core of Indigenous identities, cultural strength and ultimately, survival.

There is a struggle between obtaining the benefits of economic empowerment and maintaining the importance of family and land. In the Barunga–Wugularr region, where employment opportunities are extremely limited, low levels of full-time employment and low incomes can be attributed to Aboriginal people's decisions to stay with their families and continue to live on their traditional lands. These decisions can prevent them from gaining employment in mainstream labour markets and limit their capacity to generate income independent of government sources. Aboriginal people are aware of this. However, they are unwilling to give up the proven benefits of strong family bonds and the comfort of living on their traditional lands for the limited benefits of an increased income.

The dearth of employment opportunities within many Indigenous communities is compounded by the fact that many of the jobs on these communities are undertaken by Europeans, either in an administrative capacity, or as contractors. Some Aboriginal people resent this. Wugularr Council member Barry Weston expressed his views as follows:

> We don't want money to go outside. We want money to stay in the community. You bring builder from outside, you lose money, money go south . . . you need support, eh? I want to support my community, and kids. If old people die, you got young generation . . . two face, two different ways. I want my money to stay in my community. I just don't like money going out. For the kids. For the sport. [Money should] stay here. White man try and take Aboriginal as a blind man, but we not blind. We know, how much funding [comes in].[9]

The dilemma here lies in the availability of skills needed to produce particular outcomes. It is essential to the development of the community overall that people in jobs produce outcomes. Often local Aboriginal people do not have skills of a level sufficiently high to produce these outcomes, and in order to reach these levels they need training, which could be conducted as part of on-going projects. For example, the training of apprentices could be linked to the building of new houses as part of CDEP programmes. The continuation of the situation as it stands would appear to be intolerable.

There is a clear need to increase the educational success of Indigenous people, not just in the Barunga–Wugularr region, but throughout Australia. In 1991 only 2.2 per cent of Aboriginal and Torres Strait Islanders aged over 15 years had tertiary qualifications, compared to an average of 12.8 per cent among non-indigenous people in the same age group,[10] And about 11 per cent of Aboriginal and Torres Strait Islander people aged 15 years and over had never attended a school.[11] The 1986 figure for this in the Northern Territory was 18 per cent and almost half of those who had never attended a school were living in rural or remote areas.[12] The Barunga Community Education Centre, formerly Bamyili School, is one of eight such centres established by the Northern Territory government in order to attach post-primary facilities to existing schools. The problem is not just one of numbers, however. It is also to do with teaching in a culturally appropriate manner, something with which mainstream Australian society is still grappling.

Health and Housing

By virtually every measure, the health of Aboriginal and Torres Strait Islander people is worse than that of other Australians. Of all the world's peoples, Indigenous Australians suffer among the highest rates of diabetes, heart disease and other lifestyle diseases. The incidence of diseases relating to nutrition and to the respiratory and circulatory systems, in particular, is much greater than among the general Australian population. The result is that Aboriginal and Torres Strait Islander people are admitted to hospitals at a rate three times higher than that of other Australians and have much shorter life expectancies at birth.

The alarming state of Aboriginal and Torres Strait Islander health today is an outcome of the European invasion, which produced major changes in the diets and lifestyles of Indigenous peoples. Before invasion, Indigenous Australians had a highly mobile and healthy lifestyle, with high intakes of protein and dietary fibre and low intakes of fat, simple sugars and salt. This changed in a very short time to a much more sedentary lifestyle, with low to moderate intakes of protein, low intakes of dietary fibre and high intakes of fat, simple sugars and salt. These changes in lifestyle and diet, outlined in Table 9.1, have severely marred the health of Indigenous Australians, producing high levels of treatment and hospitalisation. For instance, at the time of the 1986 Census, Aboriginal people constituted 46 per cent of in-patients in health institutions within the Northern Territory. Kidney failure rates recorded among Aboriginal people in the Territory were seven times greater than those experienced by the non-Indigenous population and the incidence of diarrhoea and shigella was 28 times that occurring among non-Aboriginal Australians.[13] In addition, Aboriginal and Torres Strait Islander people suffered higher levels of anaemia, heart disease and dental decay than their ancestors ever did.[14] The outcome is shorter, less healthy lives.

In the early 1960s the infant mortality rate for Aboriginal babies was 100 deaths per thousand. That is, 10 per cent of these babies died before the age of five. Today, Aboriginal babies have three times the

	Hunter-Gatherer Lifestyle	**Western Lifestyle**
Physical activity level	High	Low
Principal characteristics of diet		
Energy density	Low	High
Energy intake	Usually adequate	Excessive
Nutrient density	High	Low
Nutrient composition of diet		
Protein	High	Low–moderate
Animal	High	Moderate
Vegetable	Low–moderate	Low
Carbohydrates		
Complex		High (rapidly digested)
Simple	Moderate (slowly digested)	Moderate
	Usually low (honey)	High (sucrose)
Dietary Fibre	High	Low
Fats		
Vegetable	Low	Low
Animal	Low (polyunsaturated)	High (saturated)
Sodium:Potassium ratio	Low	High

Table 9.1
Comparison of hunter-gatherer and Western lifestyles
(after O'Dea 1991)

mortality rate of other Australian babies.[15] This figure has stabilised over the last decade but does not seem to be improving. Aboriginal babies are 150–350 grams lighter at birth than their non-Indigenous counterparts and around 20per cent are recorded as having a low birth weight, less than 2500 grams.[16] Many Aboriginal infants stop growing properly after four to six months and they often suffer from acute or chronic infections. In Northern Territory communities at least 10 per cent of young children are underweight, and in some communities the figure is as high as 50 per cent.[17]

Much of the illness suffered by Indigenous children relates to poor nutritional levels. A significant proportion of the changes in diet and lifestyle since invasion can be attributed to the poor economic circumstances in which people live and the high cost of food on Aboriginal communities. The cost of fresh fruit and vegetables, in particular, is often prohibitive, even for the European people living in communities. As a consequence, children living on communities generally eat quantities of bread, chicken and stewed meat, supplemented by treats of chips, coke and ice cream, the healthier alternatives of fresh fruit and vegetables being beyond the financial reach of most Aboriginal people in Northern Territory communities. Nor is returning to a traditional diet and lifestyle a viable option, as few Indigenous people wish to take up a hunter-gatherer lifestyle. Apart from this, there are few cars in Indigenous communities (which itself is an effect of economic disadvantage) and therefore no viable way of collecting bush tucker on a regular basis. The value of this food, however, is demonstrated by a study undertaken in the early 1980s in the Kimberley. A group of ten Aboriginal people with diabetes went back to living a hunter-gatherer lifestyle and during this time their health and nutrition showed great improvement.[18] In the Barunga–Wugularr region bush foods have high status, partly because of their relative rarity and their distribution is still determined by established cultural rules.

Sick children are often hospitalised, causing disruption within families and communities. For children in the Barunga–Wugularr region, hospitalisation means being sent to Katherine, Darwin and, in some cases, Adelaide. Extended Indigenous kinship systems,

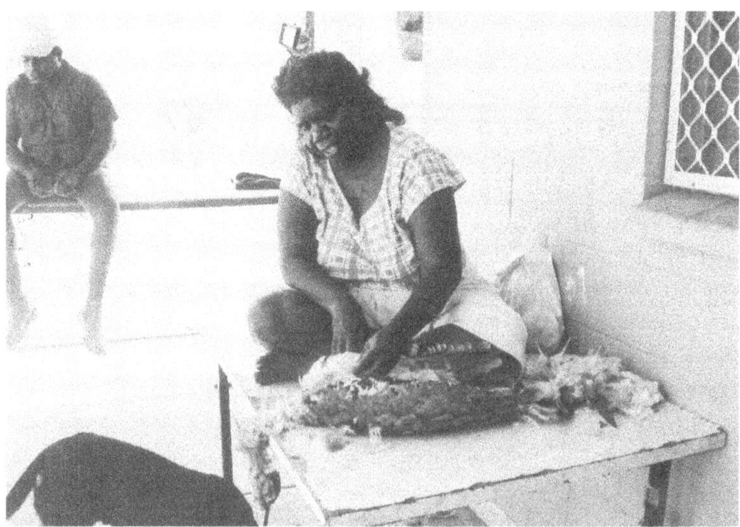

Figure 9.3
Joclyn McCarthy preparing a bush turkey,
Guy Rankin in the background, Barunga, 1994

however, offer viable methods for minimising the impact of this. The disruption caused by hospitalisation can be made worse for young children if it involves separation from their mother, so the Indigenous mother may decide to stay with the child who is in hospital. In this case, she will arrange for other members of her extended family to care for her other children, usually a sister or grandparent. The transition for the children in communities such as Barunga and Wugularr is usually smooth, as they grow up having daily contact with grandparents, aunts and uncles. The ties between extended family are close and in the Barunga–Wugularr region children will call their mother's sister 'mother'. For instance, the children of Wendy Willika call her sister 'Mummy Rachael'. Living in the same community as adults makes it easy for a sister to take over the day-to-day care of her nephews and nieces should the need arise. However, in the case of grandparents, who may not be strong themselves, caring for young grandchildren can be a physical burden, even though the responsibility may be accepted with pleasure. Extended family also offers support for those children who are sent to cities as far away as Adelaide, around 3,000 kilometres from the Barunga–Wugularr region. As noted in

Figure 9.4
Peter Manabaru, Wendy Willika (daughter of Peter's deceased wife Lily) and family members

Chapter Seven, children of the Stolen Generations, such as Lorraine Siwers, often help community members when they are sent to hospitals in far away cities. Safety nets such as these, arising from tightly knit family bonds, are not available to non-Indigenous families in the same way, as adult siblings may live in different cities, or even different countries.

One result of poor Aboriginal health is a life expectancy dramatically lower than that of other Australians. Life expectancy for Aboriginal women is 61–64 years, compared to 80.8 years for other Australian women. For Aboriginal men it is 57–60 years, and for Torres Strait Islander men 50, as against 73.9 years for other Australian men.[19] These figures reflect not only the poor health levels of Indigenous Australians but also the levels of violence in the communities in which they live. In the Northern Territory, the death rates for Aboriginal people between the ages of 20 and 45 are particularly alarming. For Aboriginal men in the 30–34 age group the rate is almost seven times higher than the equivalent rate among all other men, while the rate for Aboriginal women in the same age group is almost 13 times that recorded for all other women. Diseases of the circulatory and respiratory systems and injury or poisoning were recorded as being the dominant causes of death for both Aboriginal men and women.[20]

In an attempt to deal with these issues, the Northern Territory government has devolved control over Indigenous health issues to Indigenous organisations. This has involved the establishment of six community-controlled health care services within the Northern Territory, including the Wurli–Wurlinjang Health Service at Katherine. The Northern Territory Tripartite Forum, established in June 1991, provided the first opportunity in the history of the Territory for Aboriginal groups to have a major role in the formulation of Aboriginal health care policies.[21] In the Barunga–Wugularr region, health care is still provided primarily by European doctors and nurses, assisted by Aboriginal health care workers and supplemented by the use of bush medicines and foods. Throughout Australia there is a wide range of Indigenous medicines, the main knowledge of which is held in the custodianship of senior people. These medicines can be very effective and, in some cases, are more efficacious than Western medicines. Passing this information on from generation to generation is an important way of keeping these aspects of Aboriginal cultures alive.

The poor health of Aboriginal and Torres Strait Islanders is attributable not only to changes in diet and lifestyle, but also to environmental factors, such as housing conditions. Overall, the condition of Indigenous people's housing leaves much room for improvement. For instance, the Australian Housing Survey of 1994 found that 4 per cent of the Northern Territory's Indigenous population lived in improvised housing. While this represented an improvement from the figure of 10.3 per cent recorded in 1991, it is likely that the shift was due partly to a change in the way in which the Commonwealth government collected the data.[22] Certainly, the inadequacy of Indigenous housing can be masked by statistics. For example, Aboriginal people in the Northern Territory are recorded as having a higher proportion of owned dwellings than do non-Aboriginal people (66 per cent compared to 26 per cent). But this is not due to greater affluence, as it might at first seem. The ABS reported that:

> Most Aboriginal dwellings in this category are not comprised of conventional housing units but a variety of improvised, often rudimentary, shelters located mostly in remote rural areas and thus, are qualitatively very different.[23]

People who are economically disadvantaged have less choice in the types of housing they can afford and less income available for repairs. The condition of Indigenous housing in many parts of Australia is poor, with a high level of breakdown in household utilities such as running water, sewerage and electricity or gas. Preliminary findings from the National Housing and Infrastructure Needs Survey suggested that in some Aboriginal communities 60 per cent of kitchens were non-functional.[24] The National Aboriginal and Torres Strait Islander Survey of 1994 found that 23 per cent of the Indigenous population living in community housing in rural areas was affected by household utilities being in disrepair.[25] The study found that:

> In rural Australia at the time of the survey, an estimated 9 per cent of Indigenous households did not have a toilet in the dwelling, 7 per cent did not have electricity or gas connected, 7 per cent did not have running water connected, and 6 per cent had neither a bath or shower nor access to a communal bathroom.[26]

Figure 9.5
Peter Manabaru and visiting German artist Andreas Tschinkl at 'Riverview', the dwelling used by Peter Manabaru, Lily Willika and Paddy Babu, Barunga, 1991

The absence of such utilities can be linked to community health and well being. The breakdown in utilities is due not only to a lack of funds to pay for the costs of fixing them, but also to the greater pressure which is placed on Indigenous housing resources. In 1991, a study by the ABS found that almost half of the households in rural Aboriginal communities comprised two or more families.[27] It is likely that a comparable situation exists in the Barunga – Wugularr region.

There is no doubt that overcrowding is an important factor in environmental health. The greater the number of peoples living in a house, the greater the pressure on household resources and utilities. In Australia the Census of Population and Housing found that Indigenous households had an average number of 3.7 persons, in comparison to 2.7 for other households. The highest average number of persons was recorded for households with three families (12.6). Of those who responded to the number of bedrooms in their house, 7.2 per cent of Indigenous households recorded having more than two persons per bedroom, in comparison to 0.8 per cent of other households.[28] The average number of people per bedroom in rural areas was 1.7, considerably higher than the national average. The situation in the Barunga–Wugularr region is even worse than this. A housing survey undertaken at Wugularr in the 1990s gave a ratio of 2.53 people per bedroom, almost 50 per cent higher than the average rate for Indigenous rural communities. However, even this may be a low figure, as a recent community management plan suggested that the manner in which this figure was assessed was flawed and that the actual figure may be even higher than this.[29] Irrespective of the method of calculation used, it is clear that the average number of people per house in the Baruga–Wugularr region is intolerably high and has implications for the life span of the house. In 1992 Grant Treleavon,[30] the council book-keeper at Barunga, estimated that houses in this region had a life span of approximately five years before requiring major refurbishment. He contrasted this to an average life span of approximately fifteen years for houses owned by non-Aboriginal people, who do not place the same pressure on the resource.

To a non-Indigenous person it might seem that Indigenous people would not mind overcrowding since they place such a high importance on family relationships. In fact, the opposite is true, as overcrowding places a strain on these relationships. Indigenous people traditionally used separation as a means of resolving disputes. In a hunter-gatherer environment it was a simple matter for arguing parties to decide to live separately for a few weeks or months. This is not the case in a sedentary situation, and high levels of overcrowding exacerbate any annoyances that arise. In this situation, irritation is less likely to be suppressed and it becomes an easy matter for arguments to escalate. Thus, one social effect of overcrowding is a higher level of friction within families, with a concomitant increase in family violence.

It will be clear that much of the housing within the Barunga–Wugularr region constitutes a serious environmental health risk to its inhabitants. Many of the older houses in this region are in abysmal condition, constituting serious health hazards (and would be called shacks if owned by members of the wider Australian community). The condition of these dwellings is due not only the breakdown of household utilities but also because the majority of them are seriously overcrowded – people sleep in all parts of the houses, in the living rooms, on verandahs, and even in the yards. This has implications for their health. People sleeping outside, for instance, have a higher incidence of eye diseases arising from exposure to dust, especially during the dry season. In addition, they have a higher exposure to diseases, such as scabies, that are transferred from domestic animals.

Exacerbated by Floods

The generally poor condition of housing in this region is exacerbated by intermittent flood damage. The most serious flood of recent years was in January 1998, when most of the old low-lying residences at Wugularr were inundated. This flood also caused serious damage in the neighbouring township of Katherine, and the entire region was designated a national emergency zone. Rocky Cameron recalled:

> When that water came everybody got panicked, all of a sudden that water just came up, real quick. It was in the morning, about 7.30 a.m. People were busy in the bottom area of Wugularr, we didn't know that there was another lot of water coming up from that other end. Two lots of water coming up quick. We had to shift to that high ground. Then those little kids were having fun, swimming up and down.
>
> I stayed behind during the floods to look after the water and power. Me and Fred Blitner and a couple of others stayed behind. Everyone else was evacuated to Barunga, under doctor's orders, they might get sick if they stayed here. I didn't get sick, though. That evacuation – coppers running up and down, taking people to Barunga. They asked me 'You stopping here?' 'Yeah, I'm looking after water and power.' If that power went off I had to phone and let the Power and Water Authority know. It wasn't strange or scary with only half dozen people here. We liked it. No noise, no nothing. We didn't worry that the flood might come again. It was really quiet.[31]

Serious flooding occurred again at Wugularr in February 1999. By this time, however, the residents were practised in moving furniture and elevating perishables. Their response was one of fatalism and adjustment. The feeling of disempowerment that continues to accompany such events can be perceived in the following incident. After the 1998 floods, staff from a health-related government service entered the homes of Aboriginal residents at Wugularr and cut off the three-pin electrical plugs attached to their refrigerators, rendering the equipment unserviceable. The residents were offered no replacement or compensation and were told that this was done because the units had been flooded by polluted water. However, the refrigerator and freezer cabinets used in the community shop was dried out, cleaned and reused. Local people felt they had been discriminated against, that they had not been trusted to properly clean the refrigerators themselves. Refrigerators are a major capital purchase for any family and Wugularr people resented the scrapping of this equipment against their wishes. These actions were perceived as yet another example of abuse through short-sighted and thoughtless paternalism. This was exacerbated by the paucity of government support for re-building the community.

Figure 9.6
Flood at Wugularr, 1998
Photos courtesy Jenny Cameron and Geoff Curtis

Figure 9.7
Flood at Katherine, 1998
Photo courtesy *Katherine Times*, taken by Judy Fabian

The Social Consequences of Poverty

The social consequences of poverty in communities around the world are very similar. People who are poor and disempowered consistently seek refuge in alcohol and other drugs. Often, such people are angry with themselves, their communities and the world at large, this anger and frustration producing high incidences of vandalism, family violence and, in some cases, youth suicide. This exacerbates the normal difficulties of living, making the problems so great that it is a miracle just to survive in the present. The community profile that arises is applicable not just to Indigenous or Fourth World communities, but to all communities throughout the world that live with similar levels of economic and social disadvantage.

There exists a false perception that Indigenous Australians did not use drugs before contact with the British. In fact, Indigenous people in Australia produced and used a number of mood-altering drugs. A range of alcoholic drinks existed throughout Australia, produced from local plants and trees, and many Indigenous languages have words that refer to different types of alcohol.[32] In Tasmania alcohol was produced using the tree *Eucalyptus gunnii*, while in Queensland people made drinks from a mixture of bauhinia blossoms and wild honey.[33] In the Roper River region of the Northern Territory, which is just south of Barunga, Basedow recorded Aboriginal people as making a 'mild pandanus cider'.[34] The Europeans who saw Aboriginal people consuming these drinks commented that they became loud, merry and talkative.

Indigenous Australians used a number of native drugs, the best known of which is pituri, the dried leaves of the shrub *Duboisia hopwoodii*. The pituri plant contains nicotine and is found in the desert regions of inland Australia. Leaves from the plant were mixed with ash made by burning particular trees, especially wattles, to make a sweet and juicy mixture, similar in consistency to chewing tobacco. While pituri plants were found throughout desert environments, the plants from the Mulligan River region in south-western Queensland were highly valued as they were particularly rich in nicotine. This pituri was traded hundreds of kilometres north, south and east of the source area. Phillip King, the sole survivor of the ill-fated Burke and Wills expedition, was given pituri to allay his hunger. He commented that: 'After chewing it for a few minutes I felt quite happy and perfectly indifferent to my position'.[35]

There are important differences between Indigenous people's use of alcohol and drugs before invasion and their use in the present. Prior to invasion, Indigenous people both produced and distributed these substances. As part of their cultural responsibilities, old people controlled the allotment of these drugs and made certain that young people had limited access to them. However, the invaders brought with them commercial quantities of alcohol as well as other drugs such as opium and tobacco – in fact, the Australian government distributed tobacco to Aboriginal people in the form of rations. With their distribution no longer constrained, mood-altering drugs for the first time became available to people of both genders and most age groups. The consequences for Indigenous societies world-wide have been devastating.

To make sense of Indigenous drinking patterns, it is important to dispel some of the myths that have arisen. The first of these myths is that there are more drinkers in Indigenous communities than there are in the wider Australian community. This is just not true. As a proportion of each population, there are more Indigenous than non-Indigenous people who do not drink alcohol at all.[36] Another myth is that Aboriginal people have a genetic weakness for alcohol, that their bodies somehow absorb alcohol in different ways to that of non-Aboriginal people. This has not been proven in any studies that have been undertaken.[37] This misperception arises from two factors: the greater visibility of Indigenous drinkers and the likelihood that they will drink larger quantities of alcohol than non-Aboriginals. For example, a 1994 survey of Aboriginal people living near towns and cities showed that 42 per cent of men who were drinkers usually drank 13 or more drinks at a session, while only 3 per cent of non-Aboriginal men drank that much.[38] The intensity of Aboriginal drinking is amplified by the circumstances in which people drink, generally outdoors with a group of friends, rather than indoors by themselves. This means that drinking by Aboriginal people is more visible than that of non-Aboriginals. Also, in small communities Aboriginal people's actions have a more immediate and intense impact on their neighbours than they would in the larger and more anonymous communities in which non-Aboriginal people live. Maggie Brady's *The Grog Book* is a comprehensive and accessible study of the use of alcohol by Aboriginal people today. She concludes:

> The National Aboriginal and Torres Strait Islander Survey in 1994 found that the majority (76 per cent) of indigenous people felt that alcohol was a problem. And this is certainly true. Alcohol is associated with 75 per cent of homicides among Aboriginal people, and is involved in many assaults between husbands and wives. Alcohol use is also involved, one way or another, in disproportionately high rates of imprisonment. These are, in turn, associated with deaths in police cells or prisons.[39]

Alcohol is seen to be a problem by many people, including those living in the Barunga and Wugularr communities. It is a problem, even though each of these communities has strict regulations controlling the availability of alcohol. Spirits, known as 'hot stuff', are prohibited at both communities and the sale of beer is regulated. At Barunga, people can only buy beer after 4 p.m., at Wugularr, it can only be obtained from the local social club, which opens at 5 p.m. each day. Men are allowed six cans of beer each, while women can buy only four cans each. People who want to drink spirits or greater quantities of beer – purchased elsewhere – are required to do so before they reach a signboard, at the edge of each community, displaying the regulations prohibiting the transport of alcohol into the communities. Despite these regulations, local people get drunk regularly, especially on a Friday night. In recent years this has been augmented by the use of marijuana and, as in other communities, alcohol is involved in most incidents of family violence and heavy drinking is a direct cause of many deaths. In addition, alcohol is a factor in the alarmingly high rate of youth suicide in this region.

Alcohol is a consistent factor in the high incidences of family violence and youth suicides in some Indigenous Australian communities, including those at Barunga and Wugularr. Government attempts to deal with these issues have been made through a range of Northern Territory government initiatives, such as the Living with Alcohol programme, but the root causes, the social and economic disadvantages endured by people in these communities, are barely touched. Both family violence and youth suicide emerge from the frustration of an unsatisfactory lifestyle. Young men, in particular, are susceptible to the frustration and anger engendered by failing to reach one's potential – or even glimpsing the possibility of forming a goal, let alone hoping to reach it. Globalisation plays a role here, as young people match their own realities against the lives led by people in films and television shows. For these people, there is little opportunity for employment and incomes are low, making it difficult if not impossible to achieve the lifestyles allowed by any level of affluence. The situation is exacerbated when young men like these are placed in gaol, where there is a real risk that they will attempt suicide. The overview on the response by governments to the Royal Commission into Aboriginal Deaths in Custody contains the following observation:

> The Royal Commission investigated the deaths of 99 Aboriginal and Torres Strait Islander people in custody. In doing so it established a vivid profile of the lives of those who died – young people for the most part who had experienced unemployment, inadequate education, separation from their natural families, early contact with the criminal justice system, poor health, problems with alcohol, economic and social disadvantage.[40]

It will be evident that the circumstances outlined in this quotation are applicable to the situation existing for young people in the Barunga–Wugularr region, a situation in which suicide can be a rational choice. It can also be a protest against intolerable living conditions. This became evident at Wugularr when a succession of young people attempted to commit suicide over a period of a few weeks at the end of 1998. Two of these attempts were successful and another young man now lives out his life in a wheelchair. These young people tried to commit suicide because they had no hope for the future. And as it stands, the Australian government has made only nominal and short-term attempts to help them. Administrators look away because the problem is thought to be too difficult to solve, or is something with which Indigenous people should be able to deal themselves. Having created the parameters of the problem, the Australian government in effect abandons Indigenous people to find the solutions themselves. The link between unemployment, economic disadvantage and youth suicides was made by Bulman man Peter Lee:

> Too many young boys gone. They might just drink in the bush, kill themselves. All that trouble you know. We have to turn some around, make them good men. Put them in job.[41]

In order to deal with problems associated with the abuse of alcohol it is important to understand the social environment in which alcohol is consumed and the benefits that accrue to drinkers. Like people in other cultures, Indigenous people drink alcohol because they like it, because it has benefits for them. Certainly, alcohol helps people relax, it helps them to escape the harshness of daily living conditions and the hopelessness of the future. It helps shy people to speak out and gives normally reticent people the courage to voice their anger in situations in which they feel overwhelmed. Moreover, alcohol can be a vehicle for enjoyment, particularly when people sit together in a group; singing and having a good time, as they did in the old days. Outdoors and accompanied by singing and sometimes dancing, alcohol is consumed in a social environment that is not so different from that of ceremonial contexts. As among many Australians, alcohol can lubricate friendships. For many Aboriginal people, the lure and the evils of alcohol is exemplified in the following statement by Victor Hood:

> We [my wife and I] used to go mad, don't look after the kids because of that grog. We used to break things. We used to fight, no tucker, walking back in the hot sands [from the signboard at the edge of town], looking for tucker, asking anyone. [You should] save your money, buy your own tucker. Not grog. We used to have one little $50, that's good enough for tucker, but we got one carton of beer, looking around for modicar [to see if] we can get a lift down there [to the signboard]. Little shade, no blanket, just cardboard. We used to drink and sing a song, and dancing that corroboree. Drunken one corroborree. Good fun. Big mob used to dance – but no water, river water him long way away, we used to drink only beer. There used to be two drums of water but people bin frightened they might put something in the water, make people sick. We used to walk back and bogie la billabong. You drinking all night, make fun, sing a song – but something might be there, two men might be argi, whole lot gada fight. Another man take him partner, another boy take him partner. Then, whole lot fighting.

Domestic violence and the abuse of alcohol cause problems within families and the problem behaviours can filter down to children and teenagers, some of whom start using drugs themselves. The most damaging of these behaviours is petrol sniffing,[42] a real problem in Wugularr, though it does not take place systematically in Barunga, as indicated by Phyllis Wiynjorroc's comments:

> Some young people they get petrol along at Beswick. We don't have [that] here at Barunga. Hard one that burn up lung everywhere. Dry

up lung like that. Barunga they smoke gunja. Some bigini might take beer can and drink them.[43]

Warriors for the Lord

In the Barunga–Wugularr region, Aboriginal people often draw a distinction between 'drinkers' and 'Christian people'. The validity of this distinction was demonstrated in a recent study which correlated the relationship between the various religious beliefs and alcohol consumption for people aged 18 years and over at Wugularr.[44] This shows that the greatest deterrent to alcohol consumption is membership of either the Australian Inland Mission or Christian Fellowship, with 75 per cent of people in this category being identified as non-drinkers. It would appear that the major influence here is being a member of the Fellowship, as 74 per cent of people who identified as belonging to this group also stated that they do not drink alcohol on a regular basis. This figure is much higher than the 42 per cent non-drinking rate that was obtained for people who adhere only to traditional beliefs.

Young members of the Christian Fellowship call themselves 'Warriors for the Lord'. The success of this Fellowship, which constitutes one third of the Wugularr community, can be attributed to a number of factors. First, being a member of the Fellowship puts people in a social environment in which it is much easier to resist drinking – the social pressure is on not drinking, rather than the opposite. Second, the way in which the Fellowship meetings are structured is consistent with traditional cultural practices. In contrast to AIM services, which are performed by a minister who preaches to a seated congregation, Fellowship meetings are held outdoors and involve singing and dancing by all members of the community. They are advertised throughout the community over a public address system and meetings often continue into the small hours of the morning. Social segregation by gender is reinforced not only by placing men and women in different areas but also by each gender having particular actions adapted from traditional dance movements. From this viewpoint, Fellowship meetings can be interpreted as an extension of traditional Aboriginal corroborees; as a continuation of the flourishing ceremonial and cult life recorded in the 1960s by Maddock.[45] The meetings, however, can be noisy and disruptive, as they often continue until the early hours of the morning, and involve the use of a microphone and amplifier. Some local people find this irritating, while others don't greatly mind. Victor Hood stated:

> Fellowship, him new way, because they bin reading Bible. Him still gonna change. Might be some people grow up, I don't know how long. Every house, one always gaddim music from that tape, television, over there they got every night keyboard and loudspeaker for that Fellowship. Yeah, him keep you awake but that make all the people happy. I'm quite happy for the people, trying to help us. You can't say 'I don't want that music, that Fellowship. You can't say'. They don't drink. They [are] like me, like my son. He don't drink. I'm happy for my son.
>
> [When I was young] we only bin have a church. One bloke, he bin come. Him doing job like that one at Barunga, Mr Irwin. Him talk la church and ola people listen, insidewei. That Fellowship, they have him outside, to bring in people from every country [Mielli, Rembarrnga, etc.], ola place, because that time coming here, that change from 1999 to 2000, him coming up now. This mob try. They don't force people to come. They gada just come on their own.[46]

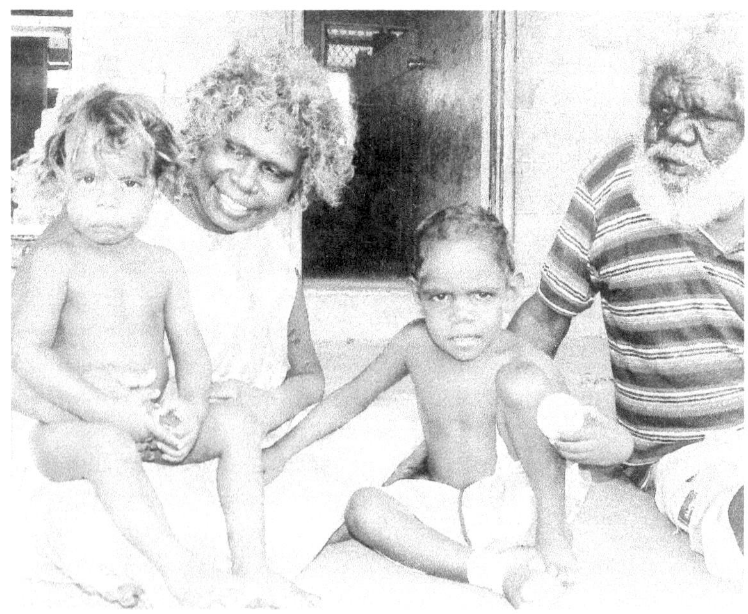

Figure 9.8
Victor Hood, wife Irene and children

Two Laws

Indigenous Australians live with two sorts of law: the criminal justice system and Indigenous customary law, Each system presenting its own assurances, problems and possibilities. A major development over the past decade has been increased community participation in the legal process and, more generally, a greater recognition of the customary laws and traditions of Aboriginal people as a source of Australian law.[47]

During the 1980s it became clear that the proportion of Aboriginal and Torres Strait Islander deaths in police custody or prison far exceeded the proportion of Aboriginal and Torres Strait Islanders in the total population. The Indigenous proportion of the total population has been between 1 and 2 per cent over the last few decades. Between 1980 and 1987 the proportion of Aboriginal deaths to total deaths in custody ranged from 11 per cent to 26 per cent.[48] The situation in the Northern Territory was found to be particularly deplorable, with Aboriginal people accounting for 73 per cent of prisoners,[49] even though they numbered only 28.5 per cent of the total population.[50] In response to this situation the Australian government established the Royal Commission into Aboriginal Deaths in Custody (RCADIC) in 1987. The commission inquired into the particular circumstances surrounding each of the 99 Aboriginal deaths in custody that had occurred between 1980 and 1989. It also inquired into the social, cultural and legal issues underlying those deaths. In 1991 the commission issued a five-volume nationally circulated report containing 339 recommendations.

The Royal Commission into Aboriginal Deaths in Custody brought these matters into public consciousness, and announced two major findings. The first of these was that many, if not all, of the deaths were related to avoidable factors, such as custodial health and safety and the Australian government's failure to comply with international obligations in regards to custodial conditions.[51] The second finding was that Indigenous Australians were not dying in disproportionate numbers *vis-à-vis* the total prison population. The high number of Indigenous deaths in custody was due to the high incarceration rates of Indigenous people. The greater proportion of Indigenous people gaoled meant that a greater proportion of the Indigenous population was at risk of dying in custody.

The Royal Commission attributed the gross over-representation of Aboriginal and Torres Strait Islander peoples in police custody or prison to two main factors. First, the operation of the criminal justice system was such that Aboriginal people had a disproportionately greater chance of coming into contact with that system. It found that Aboriginal people were more likely to be sought by police, more likely to be charged rather than cautioned, more likely to be arrested, less likely to be granted bail and when convicted to have fewer suitable sentencing options. Taken together, these factors form a systematic system of discrimination. The RCADIC proposed a significant number of recommendations aimed at reforming the operation of the criminal justice system.

Second, the RCADIC attributed the disproportionate number of Aboriginal people in custody to a deprivation of their political and economic power to control their own lives, which had led to disadvantage and inequality in such areas as housing, health and education. The commission emphasised the importance of self-determination in addressing these issues:

> The thrust of this report is that elimination of disadvantage requires an end of domination and an empowerment of Aboriginal people; that control of their lives, of their communities must be returned to Aboriginal hands.[52]

One of the RCADIC's recommendations was that an independent evaluation be conducted of the Northern Territory Department of Correctional Services Community Justice Scheme, with the aim of examining options for enabling Indigenous forms of social control to operate in Aboriginal communities with the formalised cooperation of the Australian legal system.[53] During 1993 the Department of Correctional Services canvassed Indigenous people's opinions of court and sentencing procedures. The review committee was addressed by Cyril McCartney, President of Barunga–Mayallaluk Community Government Council, in September 1993. McCartney stated that Aboriginal people wanted to be involved in court and sentencing procedures, and emphasised the importance of courts taking into account first-hand information from residents.[54] In 1993, at the request of Council, the local court was convened at Barunga – for the first time the views of Aboriginal community members were taken into account when determining sentences.

It is sometimes argued that offences by Indigenous people against their peers should be tried according to customary law, since European punishments often do not effectively deal with Indigenous offences. Gaol sentences do not deter the majority of offenders, boys and young men under 20 years of age,[55] and fines often are paid by relations. Moreover, for serious offences such as murder, punishment by European law does not preclude punishment by Aboriginal law. Once the offender leaves gaol they still have to face the discipline of customary law. However, customary law may not adequately address some issues, such as the very high rate of violence against women.[56] There are many important differences between criminal law and customary law. According to Aboriginal people in the Barunga–Wugularr region the main difference is that Aboriginal law is much tougher. This view is expressed by the senior traditional owner of the Barunga–Wugularr region, Phyllis Wiynjorroc:

> Aboriginal law, him really hard. Him hard like a rock. Aboriginal law doesn't change all the time like that mununga [whitefella] law. Aboriginal law really hard.[57]

This perception of Aboriginal customary law as impersonal and unchanging is important to its effective implementation. The general view is that ancestors laid down Indigenous law during the creation era and that this law cannot be changed. As such, the law is thought to be impartial – hard, but fair. This idea is not diminished by the fact that customary law has to be interpreted by living people who will have their own family affiliation and biases. Flexibility is built into customary law partly because it is interpreted and partly because it takes into account the possibility of intervention by the spirit world. The latter can support an argument that the people involved in the crime should not be held personally responsible. For example, one young man was exonerated from responsibility for a fatal car accident on the grounds that immediately prior to the accident he saw a devil's hand take control of the wheel. When the question of punishment arose, members of his family successfully argued his innocence on these grounds. Another difference between customary law and criminal law is that the former does not have the notion of a criminal record. Once a matter has been dealt with it is considered finished.[58]

The adaptability of Aboriginal law and the manner in which it can work in tandem with the criminal justice system can be seen in an incident related by Jimmy Wessan, a senior man at Wugularr:

> Some young boys from Bulman they stole that Council Toyota. They drove it down here [to Wugularr] and they bin run out of diesel on that ceremony ground. That modicar it stopped right on that ceremony ground. Next day they said 'We gotta get that modicar'. I said 'You can't have that modicar. That belongs to old men now. That's a culture car now'.[59]

The people who owned the car reported the theft and policemen came to Wugularr in search of it. Jimmy Wessan told them what had happened and that the car was now a culture car. The policemen decided that this matter was Aboriginal business and that they would not interfere. Indigenous law took over in ascribing cultural rules for riding in that car. The main rules were that only Yirrtija men who were custodians for the surrounding countryside could ride in it and that it could not carry women. The latter ruling was particularly troublesome since the car had been stolen from the Women's Resource Centre in Bulman. The women from the Centre came to Wugularr and offered to buy the car back, first for $1,000 and then $4,000 but the old men said the car could not be sold. They said that the car was theirs now, since it had been left on the ceremony ground. That was the law.

There have been both positive and negative developments over the past decade. On the positive side is an increased concern by the Australian judiciary with Indigenous perceptions of criminal justice matters, a greater recognition of Indigenous customary laws, an increase in the implementation of alternative dispute resolutions and the emergence of more culturally appropriate sentencing patterns. For example, rather than being gaoled, people in the Barunga–Wugularr region who are guilty of minor offences may be sentenced to community service at dry locales, such as Manyallaluk and Bulman, or to undertaking cultural training out bush, away from the temptations of community living. Jimmy Wesan argues that learning culture can help to deal with the problems of young people:

> Next year, I'm going to sound up that ceremony with my nephew Phillip, Joe, old Jimmy Hood there and old Victor Hood. I'm going to stand up for them and biggest mob will come. That young mob, that kid, if they make trouble, too much this one, too much smoke, we are going to put them in that ceremony for maybe 4, 5, 6 month, like that. Some young fellows, so they can forget about [petrol sniffing, smoking

> drugs, teasing old people]. Some young fellows, that's why I'm going to do like that. They might say 'alright, we turn around to bisnus side now'.[60]

This quotation highlights the contrasts between the criminal law system and Indigenous law. In the former the emphasis is punitive, but Indigenous customary law aims to help minor offenders 'turn around' and become functioning members of the community. The increased recognition of the validity of customary law and the development of localised and effective community-based justice schemes has been an important facet of the empowerment of Aboriginal communities. Judging by the current political climate and discussions which are now taking place within the Australian judiciary, it is likely that future developments will include an increased concern with Aboriginal perceptions of criminal justice matters and a greater recognition of, and reference to, customary laws.

In contrast, legislative changes in the Northern Territory and Western Australia have had a negative impact on Indigenous Australians. The Northern Territory Chief Minister, Shane Stone promoted the notion of 'Zero Tolerance Policing', pioneered in New York, as a tough and uncompromising approach to low-level crime, disorderliness and quality-of-life issues. One result is the increased incarceration of Indigenous offenders. Further, both the Northern Territory and Western Australia have introduced legislation which allows mandatory imprisonment of juveniles convicted of certain offences. This legislation effectively discriminates on the basis of race, since it targets offences that are most commonly committed by Indigenous people. The tragic consequence of such laws was highlighted in February 2000 by the suicide in custody in Darwin of a 15 year old boy from an Aboriginal community in a very remote part of the Northern Territory. The boy was serving a 28-day sentence for an offence concerning minor damage in his community and the theft of pens, felt-tip pens and pencils.[61] These matters were highlighted by the Aboriginal and Torres Strait Island Commision (ATSIC) in a recent report to the United Nations Human Rights Committee:

> Northern Territory data show clearly that mandatory sentencing has an overwhelming impact on Aboriginal people rather than non-Aboriginal people. This relates in part to the types of offence included and excluded from the mandatory regimes. For example, the types of

> property offences, such as fraud, excluded form the mandatory sentencing regimes are precisely the offences where the majority of offenders are non-Indigenous.[62]

These legislative actions on the part of the Northern Territory and Western Australia have led to an increase in Aboriginal imprisonment, exacerbating an already intolerable situation. Despite the findings and recommendations of the RCIADIC, there continues to be gross over-representation of Indigenous prisoners in Australian gaols and the continuing high level of Indigenous deaths in custody. Aboriginal people are still 12 times more likely to be incarcerated than non-Indigenous Australians.[63] ATSIC attributes this to a failure on the part of Australian States and Territories to commit to the genuine implementation of key recommendations of the Royal Commission:

> The failure to improve the situation in respect of deaths in custody also relates at a fundamental level to the failure to acknowledge the right of self-determination for Indigenous peoples. This relates to both the inadequate regard given to the need for negotiation and self-determination in relation to the design and delivery of services, and, more broadly, to the failure to deal effectively with the underlying problems identified by the RCIADIC.[64]

Deprivation of the political and economic power to control their own lives is the main underlying problem identified by the Royal Commission into Aboriginal Deaths in Custody – factors central to the issues discussed in this chapter. At this stage in the history of Indigenous communities, it is clear that any kind of viable future will have to be moulded according to Indigenous agendas. The role of government agencies will have to change from being the designers of Indigenous destinies to being the facilitators of a future shaped by Indigenous peoples themselves.

Ten

A Traditional Future

I would ask the reader to remember this . . . that the paintings are not just beautiful pictures. They are about Aboriginal law, Aboriginal life. They are also about our resistance over the past 200 years, and our refusal to forget the land of our Ancestors. They are about cultural, social and political survival. You can't get any clearer statement than that.

Galarrwuy Yunupingu[1]

That picture you can see but that story him secret.

David Blanarsi[2]

This book documents a history of changing relations between Aboriginal and non-Aboriginal people in the Barunga–Wugularr region of Australia. This is viewed through the era of policies of protection and assimilation, to the contemporary movement towards self-determination and reconciliation. Early European administrative policies were explicitly interventionist, with statutory powers controlling the movements and places of residence of Aboriginal people. For much of the twentieth century these policies were implemented with the conscious intention of undermining traditional Aboriginal social structures in order to at first achieve general community compliance, and later in order to facilitate the integration of younger generations into mainstream European society. This was followed by policies acknowledging the rights of Aboriginal peoples to self-determination. Aboriginal people responded by adjusting the more mutable facets of their own social relationships in order to ensure the continuance of the basic principles that structure their daily lives. And yet, despite the many direct incursions by Europeans, it is clear that a distinctly Indigenous world view has endured.

It would be naive, however, to think of Aboriginal people as passive victims of colonisation. This notion is based on the stereotype that Indigenous peoples are so tied to the ways of the past that they are unable to shape their cultures to adjust to new challenges and situations. This view fails to recognise that Indigenous societies are dynamic and flexible, possessing a creative ability to generate new variants of cultural practices and to transform their cultures in strategic ways.[3] Once the violence of frontier contact had passed, Aboriginal people actively sought to change particular aspects of their lives. Emerging from a history of connectedness and armed with a flexible and sophisticated understanding of social process, they were well adapted to exploit the possibilities of new situations.

Globalisation offers new opportunities to Australia's indigenous peoples but also poses fresh threats. On the one hand, globalisation provides Indigenous people with new tools for advancing their own agendas, transforming hegemonic social and political orders and for engaging the wider world in the value of their cultural knowledge and practices. On the other hand, globalistion has the potential to extend the process of colonisation, giving rise to a new invasion. For many non-Indigenous people, globalisation is simply a means to open up new markets and to find new ways of 'selling' Indigenous culture. There is little understanding of the rules governing Indigenous cultural and intellectual property, or of Indigenous culture as a living heritage. The result is that Indigenous people are having to fight harder on a variety of fronts to ensure their cultural survival and to find new means of asserting their rights and autonomy. A key issue here is control – control over land, control over knowledge, control over the past, present and future. The object of the struggle is not only contemporary Indigenous cultures, but also the future of Indigenous societies themselves.

Linguistic Diversity

The linguistic diversity of the Barunga–Wugularr region is today manifest in the mobile populations that move throughout the territories associated with all the language groups within the region. In particular, there are strong kinship and social alliances with other Aboriginal people in western and central Arnhem Land. The main language groups living in the Barunga–Wugularr region today are those of the Jawoyn, Mangarrai, Mara, Mielli, Ngalkpon and Rembarrnga. The settlements at Bulman, Weemol and Gropulyu are located on Ngarrbun land and are inhabited mostly by Rembarrnga, Ngalkpon and Mielli people. Taken together, these form a complex web of family, social and linguistic inter-relationships.

Aboriginal communities throughout northern Australia are

bilingual. English is a second language, while Kriol is the *lingua franca.* Kriol is the Aboriginal creole spoken by more than 15,000 people in northern Australia.[4] To the outsider it sounds very much like English, since many of the words derive from that language. However, the structure of the language – the way it is put together – derives from Aboriginal language structures. Kriol is not a bastardised form of English but a full language with the ability to convey the full range of complex ideas that are part of Indigenous societies in northern Australia.

The linguistic versatility is an example of the sophistication of Aboriginal social systems and has always been a normal part of existence for Aboriginal people. Prior to contact, people in northern Australia usually spoke two or three languages, and even today senior people can speak two or three Aboriginal languages as well as Kriol and some English. While young people as a rule know only a selective range of words in Aboriginal languages, they all speak English as a second language and Kriol as their mother tongue. While these children are routinely bilingual, old people lament the loss of traditional languages. Jimmy Wesan comments on this matter:

> I worry a little bit about that way now. Even this time when we try and talk with kid, we try and talk language. They can't listen. They've got to follow that European way. They don't even listen. But our law they sort of forget about it. They aren't interested in the language. They are going to go European way now. Can't do nothing about it, anyway. Oh my kid all right, little bit. I keep talking that language a little bit. They understand a little bit. They understand what we talk but they don't answer back. They say munanga way now 'Yes, yes.' Our father, mother, they used to talk with us and we would answer back with language. Little boy or little girl would talk back with language then. But now they say 'Yes, yes', every time with munanga language.[5]

The impetus to speak Kriol and English, rather than 'language' arose when people from different language groups left Arnhem Land to live near Maranboy or Beswick station. This was a pragmatic response to the linguistic challenges of a new situation, as outlined by Anita Camfoo:

> Since all different people from different languages used to work there, the only language they would communicate in was Kriol. That's where

> Kriol was formed. So, you know, a Rembarrnga person had to speak to a person from Arnhem Land, Rithangu tribe. That's where our people used to borrow words from, you know, white people and just make up their own language, you know, and then the Kriol was formed.[6]

Unless there is a major initiative to conserve Aboriginal languages such as Ngalkpon or Jawoyn, this situation is unlikely to change. As it stands, there are no longer sufficient numbers of people speaking these languages for them to have a viable future. Moreover, these languages no longer serve a purpose. There is little contemporary value in distinguishing people through linguistic differentiation. As Peter Manabaru says, 'We are one language now. One language and one people.'[7] Furthermore, the original purpose of Kriol, that of cross-cultural communication between different Aboriginal language groups, is unchanged.

Another linguistic change in this region relates to the relationship between place of residence and language group. Since both the Barunga and Wugularr communities are located on the Bugula clan lands of the Jawoyn people, it might be expected that Jawoyn would be the largest language group in these contemporary settlements. This, however, is not the case, as is indicated in Table 9.1. In fact, in May 1999 there were only seven Jawoyn people living at Wugularr, representing only 1.5 per cent of the total population. The largest language group is Rembarnnga, with 118 community members, or 24 per cent of the population. The next largest language group is Ngalkpon, followed by Rithangu. All other language groups are represented by very small numbers, with none having a maximum of more than nine community members. While the exact numbers for the community at Barunga were not recorded at the time of writing, the pattern there is broadly similar, though it is likely that the most populous language group at Barunga is Ngalkpon, rather than Rembarrnga. Again, there are very few Jawoyn people living at Barunga, although there are more there than at Wugularr.

Despite a drastic drop in the proportion of Jawoyn people living in this area, there is continuity in the ways in which Aboriginal rights to land are maintained. The most likely incursion upon such relationships relates to the increasingly small numbers of Jawoyn people living at Barunga and Wugularr. However, this is in no way thought to diminish the ownership rights of Jawoyn people

Language Group	Number	Percentage of population
Jawoyn	7	1.5
Ngalkpon	79	17.5
Rembarrnga	108	23.8
Mielli	70	15.5
Mara	9	1.9
Rithangu	24	5.3
Mudburra	7	1.5
Jingli	5	1.0
Woyala	2	0.5
Mangurai	1	0.3
Walpiri	1	0.3
Not known	138	31.0
Total	**451**	**100.0**

Table 10.1
Wugularr Community Profile
According to Language Group, 1999

over this land. Both communities are located on Bagula clan lands and the senior Bagula person, Phyllis Wiynjorroc, is clearly identified as senior traditional owner and 'boss' of these lands. Phyllis Wiynjorroc lives at Barunga but visits Wugularr regularly and has a daughter living permanently at Wugularr, providing a family presence in the community. Phyllis appointed a local man, Victor Hood, to act as her proxy at Wugularr. He is a senior Mielli man of Dhuwa moiety and the Wamut skin group and is classificatory brother to Phyllis's skin group, which is Wamutjan, in Ngalkpon terms. This means that Victor is of the appropriate moiety and skin group to take on ownership responsibilities for Bagula clan lands in this area. His role is that of overseeing the routine cultural management of the area but he consults, and is directed by, Phyllis Wiynjorroc if potentially contentious issues arise. Thus, traditional power structures are maintained and adapted for the requirements of a new situation.

Caring for Country

While much has changed for Aboriginal people, social structures and cultural codes based on Aboriginal laws are still the guiding principles of existence. Caring for country is one of the core responsibilities of

Aboriginal people but people's ability to do this well has been adversely affected since invasion, due mainly to changing settlement patterns. Prior to invasion Barunga people knew their country thoroughly. They were able to look after it on a continuous basis as they moved throughout the land. This would include lighting fires to keep the country 'clean', holding appropriate ceremonies, making rock art and, where necessary, renewing rock paintings. Contact has disrupted this pattern, as people now live more sedentary lives. These activities are performed less frequently and are more likely to occur near permanent settlements. Cultural continuity nevertheless exists simply in the performance of these tasks.

One of the most important ways in which people keep their culture strong is through caring for country. This is based on a detailed knowledge of land and the animals and plants that inhabit it, as well as a deep understanding of the role that Aboriginal people have to play to keep their country alive. As they move through their lands they pay attention to the nuances of seasonal and ecological information that the land provides for them. When Aboriginal people are travelling they use this knowledge to obtain food and water, find materials for making paintings and baskets and to navigate a safe trip. Aboriginal people inhabit landscapes that are full of meaning, that are inherently powerful and potentially dangerous. There is a strong sense of the country being aware of, and responsive to, the actions of Aboriginal people. Such a view of country is evident in the following discussion with Paddy Fordham Wainburranga:

> We used to make our camp sometimes without water. Then early in the morning we'd get up and sing out and look at the country carefully, so we could find water and go hunting.
>
> That's what this part of Arnhem Land is like. Other places are all right but here in the middle you've got to talk to your country. You can't just travel quiet, no! Otherwise, you might get lost, or have to travel much further. That's the law for the centre of Arnhem Land. For Rembarrnga people.
>
> My father used to do it. We used to get up early in the morning and he'd sing out and talk. Sometimes he didn't talk early in the morning, only when travelling and we used to stop and he'd talk then in language.
>
> It would make you look carefully at the country, so you could see the signs, so you could see which way to go . . .

> The law about singing out was made like that to make you notice that all the trees here are your countrymen, your relations. All the trees and birds are your relations.
>
> There are different kinds of birds here. They can't talk to you straight up. You've got to sing out to them so they can know you . . .
>
> That's why I talked to the birds this morning, and all the birds were happy. All the birds were really happy and sang out: 'Oh! That's a relation of ours. That's a relation we didn't know about'. That's the way they spoke, and they were happy to sing out.[8]

While all Aboriginal people have a responsibility to learn about and care for their own country, senior custodians bear the responsibility for important communal aspects of country. In the Barunga–Wugularr region, non-Jawoyn people undertake this management, as there are few Jawoyn people living in these areas who are of the appropriate social categories to take on custodial responsibilities. Many of the Jawoyn custodians for this land have died or moved to other parts of Jawoyn country and Aboriginal people's response to this has been for other language groups to take over responsibility for important parts of Jawoyn country. Paddy Fordham Wainburranga discusses this matter:

> It's Bagula clan country. It belongs to old Lamjerroc. We've got the junggayi here. We've got two of my relations. We're taking over responsibility. Jack Chadum and Peter Manabaru.[9]

This process is not new. Since the 1940s or earlier, Ngalkpon people have had a role in looking after Jawoyn rock sites and ceremonies in this region, as noted by Macintosh.[10] These actions show how traditional social structures have adapted to the changes occurring in the circumstances of Aboriginal people in this region. In particular, it is clear that the junggayi relationship takes precedence over membership of a language group when it comes to the custodial role integral to caring for country. When there were few, or no, suitable Jawoyn people in the immediate region to look after land and ceremonies correctly, senior people of the right categories in neighbouring language groups were called upon to assist. The over-riding principle was co-operation rather than conflict and the delineation of cultural or physical territory. This was an extension of the roles and interconnections already established in regional ceremonies.[11]

Cultural Life

A concern with connectedness is inherent in the cultural lives of Indigenous Australians. Grounded in laws established in the ancestral past, contemporary cultural life shapes the futures of Aboriginal people. In the Barunga–Wugularr region it has endured the many incursions by Europeans, who recognised ceremonial activity as a rallying point for traditional beliefs and social structures, and so targeted these things for eradication. Aboriginal people reacted by adjusting the more mutable facets of their own social relationships in order to ensure continuance of the basic principles that structure their daily lives. Some rules were bent, some perhaps forgotten, but the fundamental social structures and cultural laws, clearly grounded in Aboriginal systems of knowledge, have endured.

A crucial way by which people are connected to the world around them is through travel, arising from a history of connectedness and relating primarily to kinship and ceremonial obligations. There is much movement of people within the lands of this region, with continuous social exchanges between people within settlements in the Barunga–Wugularr region as well as between Barunga people and other Aboriginal people from places such as Oenpelli in western Arnhem land and Maningrida in north-central Arnhem Land. Ceremonies are held every year within the Barunga–Wugularr region and people will travel several hundred kilometres in order to attend ceremonies in their traditional country. The ceremonies, which are held on a regular basis, include a series of *lorrkon* rituals associated with the calling in and proper dispersal in the landscape of the spirits of dead people, and a range of ceremonial cycles called the *Maraian*, *Jabuduruwa* and *Gunapippi*. In recent years people have held these ceremonies in the Bulman area in central Arnhem Land, where there is little likelihood of disruption by those under the influence of alcohol.

The initiation of young boys is an important ritual that can absorb a large percentage of a family's resources. This ceremony has to be performed by a large number of people over a period of about two weeks and involves a core group of around twenty dancers, each of whom have to be cared for and fed by the families of the boys being initiated. In a community with a very low average income, this involves much planning and ingenuity, as well as calls upon the resources of extended family. Often, people simply cannot afford the cost of the ceremony. In these cases a doctor at the hospital conducts the medical part of the initiation ceremony and the cultural information is passed to the child in a more *ad hoc* manner. Dwayne Kennedy, pictured in Figure 9.1 with his father Richard Kennedy, was lucky to have a traditional initiation. The fact that his mother was a practising nurse meant the family was able to bear the financial costs of the ceremony. There is a certain irony here in that the people who are most able to succeed within the Western system are best positioned to pay for traditional ceremonies.

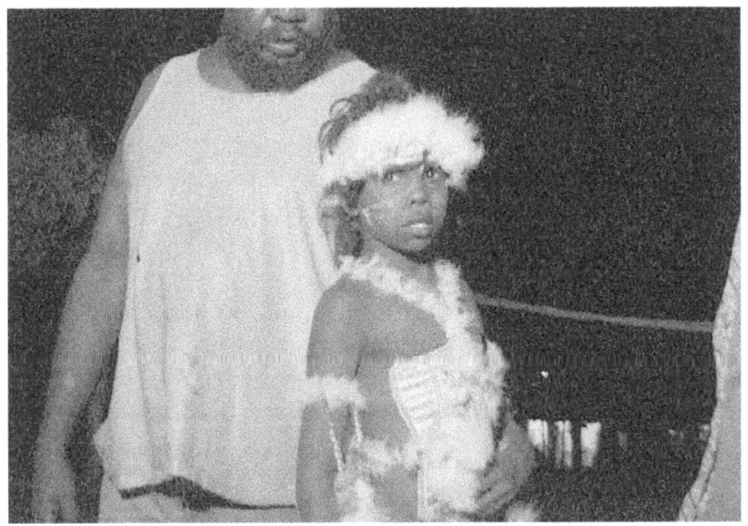

Figure 10.1
Dwayne Kennedy at his initiation ceremony, Wugularr, May 1999

The cultural life of Barunga people is embedded in the rules established in an ancestral past that upholds and structures the negotiations of the present. In this way, contemporary ceremonies integrate both 'old ways' and 'new ways'. For example, the final stages of a *lorrkon* ceremony once included the disposal of the bones of the dead in the burial pole itself. Today, bodies are buried with a Christian-style service and only their close personal possessions are placed in the *lorrkon*. These are changes of degree, rather than kind. The content of the ceremony itself appears to be substantially unchanged since before invasion and is described in such terms by Barunga people.

An important artistic practice associated with burial rituals is the painting of the substantive physical structures associated with the deceased, such as their house and the larger trees surrounding it, with red ochre. This traditional practice is incorporated into contemporary social circumstances and is sometimes used on cars as well as dwellings. The finger marks help the dead person's spirit to disperse, but they also show that they were closely associated with the vehicle or house.

Aboriginal people often draw a distinction between 'corroborees' and 'business'. Corroborrees are ceremonies that can be viewed by all members of the community. They include the open sections of mortuary ceremonies, in which the spirits of dead people are laid to rest. Business, on the other hand, refers to ceremonies which are conducted by senior people and which can only be viewed by people of the same gender. Both 'women's business' and 'men's business' exist. However, it is men's business that is most commonly performed in the present. These include special songs, dances and body paintings, each of which is specific to the particular ceremony.

Most ceremonies involve both men and women, though they take on quite different roles within the ceremony itself, and there are sections of some ceremonies that are undertaken by men in isolation. For example, ceremonial *lorrkon* are produced and painted in a restricted, male-only context, though they are open to viewing by everyone in the Aboriginal community as part of the *lorrkon* series of ceremonies. In these circumstances, women and children wait at the local community, usually playing cards or resting, until it is time for them to actively participate in the ceremony. However, they also undertake preparatory activities, such as the cooking of damper and tea for the men who are working on ceremonial business. It is important that women see men's body paintings and Maddock[12] recalls that sometimes men would touch up their paintings in order to give the women and children 'a good show'. Peter Manabaru states that:

> When the men got the paint on . . . men allowed to go down with that painting from the ceremony for that woman to have a look, proper way . . . they got to look . . . they got to see the paintings.[13]

In contrast, women have ceremonies from which men are totally excluded. In these circumstances there appears to be no principle that states that men should view women's body paintings. This suggests a level of autonomy for women's ceremonies not found in those run by men. However, women's ceremonies are rarely enacted today, even though men's ceremonies are held annually. It may be that women's ceremonies are thought to be less central to the contemporary social identities of Aboriginal people in the region.

While there is much continuity, there have been substantial changes in the ways in which individuals create their social identities. One identifiable change relates to the way in which the idea of clan, which is linked to inherited tracts of land, is used in the construction of identity. Up until the recent past, clan was an important means of identifying an individual. In reference to Ngalkpon people living at Barunga during the 1960s and 1970s, Maddock[14] argues that the significance of clan and clan species for personal identity is suggested by the practice of speaking of or to a person by the name of his clan or its species. Such a practice occurs only rarely in contemporary Barunga society. In fact, information on the clan to which someone belongs is not as well known as other types of information relating to social identity. Such information can usually only be obtained directly from the person themselves, rather than from other members of the community. Likewise, children and younger people are often unaware of their clan affiliation though they will usually know the moiety, skin and language groups to which they belong.

The question arises as to why the identifier of clan might be particularly vulnerable to change. The answer lies in the specificity of clan in relation to relatively small and defined tracts of land and to the problems involved in visiting these areas. Once they became permanently based in the immediate vicinity of Barunga and Wugularr it became virtually impossible for many Ngalkpon people to visit their clan lands. This was a problem of long-standing by the 1960s and Maddock[15] comments that some of the young men who accompanied him on his trips into central Arnhem Land were visiting their traditional lands for the first time. The social identifier of clan may also have come under pressure through the general acceptance of marriages that are 'wrong' in terms of skin-group classifications. The interesting issue at this point in the history of the region is how the resettlement of central Arnhem Land through the outstation movement, combined with the greater availability of four-wheel-drive vehicles, will affect the use of clan lands. This may have subsequent influence on the use of clan as a form of social identity.

Another alteration that has arisen in the recent past relates to the social identifier of semi-moiety, which is inherited patrilineally. This was a significant social classification during the time that Maddock was at Barunga and it was important to the correct enactment of certain ceremonies that the son take on the semi-moiety of the father.[16] However, the classification of semi-moiety is rarely mentioned today. This may be due partly to the different forms of information given to a male researcher in the 1960s and a female researcher in the 1990s but it is also possible that this social category is becoming less central to Barunga social life. Maddock[17] comments that during the 1960s there existed conflict between the principles governing this and other forms of classification. It is likely that any pressure that did exist on this type of social identifier would have been exacerbated by the increase in 'wrong' marriages, since this would confuse the cultural laws governing the inheritance of clan.

Conversely, it is possible to distinguish the emergence of new forms of social identifiers. One of these is the identification that comes with place of residence. In the past, people resided on their own lands, though they regularly visited their neighbours in order to participate in joint social activities, such as ceremonies. This meant that there was usually coalescence between place of residence and affiliation to territory through language group. The establishment of settlements by Europeans conflated with local Aboriginal desires to live in easy access to food and encouraged many to move away from their traditional lands. This loosened the link between place of residence and territorial affiliation through language group and allowed space for a different type of land-based affiliation, that of affiliation to place of residence. This occurs at levels other than those relating to the territory associated with particular language groups or clans. For example, people who are more concerned with the 'old way' rather than the 'new way' will often choose to live at outstations, such as Gropulyu in central Arnhem Land, rather than in larger community centres, such as Barunga or Wugularr, that are closer to the town facilities of Katherine. Nevertheless, it is important to recognise that people in the region are highly mobile and may live in a range of different community centres throughout the course of the year.

Another emerging form of social identifier is that relating to occupation, in particular that of artist. Many women and men in Barunga society today can be described in terms of their role as producers of artefacts for sale, which is unlikely to have been the case prior to the establishment of a European market for these artefacts. As Greenhalgh and Megaw[18] remark, artists as a defined and recognisable class do not exist in the societies of most, if not all, Indigenous peoples. Indeed, Berndt[19] states that none of the Aboriginal languages in Arnhem Land contain a term which encompasses the Western concept of art[20] and later he expands this to suggest that this is characteristic of all Australian Aboriginal languages.[21] Unlike art in Western societies, the art of Aboriginal people is rarely, if ever, produced solely for its aesthetic value.[22]

Figure 10.2
Peter Manabaru preparing didgeridoos, Barunga, 1994

While the production of art for a non-Indigenous market is one of the chief ways in which Barunga people are able to earn money, this does not mean that cultural rules and parameters do not inform this production. The production of this art is grounded in long-established political and religious associations, in particular those associated with land. The creation of art is a direct way of linking to the Dreaming, irrespective of where the artwork finally ends up. One thread clearly linking both male and female artists who produce on a regular basis is the extent of their religious knowledge

Figure 10.3
Bangardi painting a didgeridoo, Barunga, 1992

and their central roles in ceremonies. Even art produced in informal contexts is linked to the ideological sphere in such a way that does not leave room for the Western concept of art produced purely for its own sake. As in other parts of Australia,[23] Barunga artists do not draw a line between the economic imperative to produce goods to earn money and the cultural imperative to sustain traditions, skills and cultural competencies.

The Barunga Festival

The other way in which Aboriginal people engage with others outside the communities in which they live is through regional festivals. These are important annual events in many parts of Aboriginal Australia and include the Laura Cultural Festival, Yuendumu Sports Weekend and the Barunga Sport and Cultural Festival. As Brett points out, such events are a new form of 'ceremony', an extension of the large meetings that are a long established part of cultural interactions within a region:

> For such events people travel long distances to attend in much the same way as they did for traditional religious ceremonies. These 'Western' festivities have been utilised to get large groups of people together in a form of celebration.[24]

Reflecting the contemporary interests of Aboriginal people in northern Australia, the Barunga Festival is a celebration of both modern and traditional life. The program includes a variety of sporting and cultural events including Australian football, boxing, men's and women's basketball, women's softball, modern Aboriginal music, traditional Aboriginal dancing, an Aboriginal arts competition and an exhibition of arts and crafts. Inter-group sport and cultural competitions reinforce existing ties between Aboriginal groups and establish new ones. They also provide Aboriginal people with an opportunity to excel, bringing pride to themselves, their families and their communities. A regular highlight is the spear-throwing competition, which integrates both sporting and cultural facets of the festival. The cultural component of the festival affirms the importance of traditional values to Aboriginal people. The performance of traditional dances, for example, gives Aboriginal people from different areas the chance to display important facets of their traditional culture to both Aboriginal and non-Aboriginal people and is a visual statement that they are 'strong in culture'.

As with traditional ceremonies, the festival reinforces ties between participating Aboriginal communities. Around 6,000 people from throughout northern Australia participate each year. Large contingents regularly attend from as far as Ernabella in the south and Snake Bay in the north, as well as from Western Australia. This inter-community festival brings together people from up to thirty Aboriginal communities for the enjoyment of sports and cultural activities. Technical and logistic support, including stage management services and umpiring and security services, are drawn from the broader Aboriginal community, not unlike the manner in which a 'custodian' will work for an 'owner' in a ceremony. The hosting of such a large gathering brings considerable prestige to the Barunga community, in the same manner that large ceremonial gatherings have always brought distinction to their host communities, for in Indigenous societies, status is obtained through giving, not through keeping resources to oneself.

In 1988, the Barunga Festival served an overtly political purpose when the Barunga Statement was handed to the Prime Minister, Bob Hawke. This statement was incorporated into a painting that was painted jointly by artists from both northern and central Australia. It called for a formal treaty between Aboriginal and non-Aboriginal Australians. The Barunga Statement follows on

Figure 10.4
Bob Hawke and Cyril McCartney at the Barunga Festival, 1988

from the success of the bark petition sent to the Commonwealth Government in Canberra by Yolngu people to assert their political rights.[25] These are examples of Indigenous peoples using art production not only as a means of sustaining and strengthening their communities, but also as a way of transforming their social and political relationships with the dominant hegemonies of colonial relationships. Like the bark petition of the Yolngu, the Barunga Statement received widespread national publicity and today a treaty is still on the national political agenda.

The Barunga Festival promotes understanding between Aboriginal and non-Aboriginal people in an informal and festive setting. Though this is neither its focus nor a particular purpose, it provides a rare opportunity for tourists and other non-Aboriginal people to visit a remote Aboriginal community and experience Aboriginal culture at first hand, without having first obtained a permit. The festival receives much positive media attention, facilitating awareness and appreciation of Aboriginal cultural identity and reinforcing social ties between Aboriginal people and the wider Australian society.

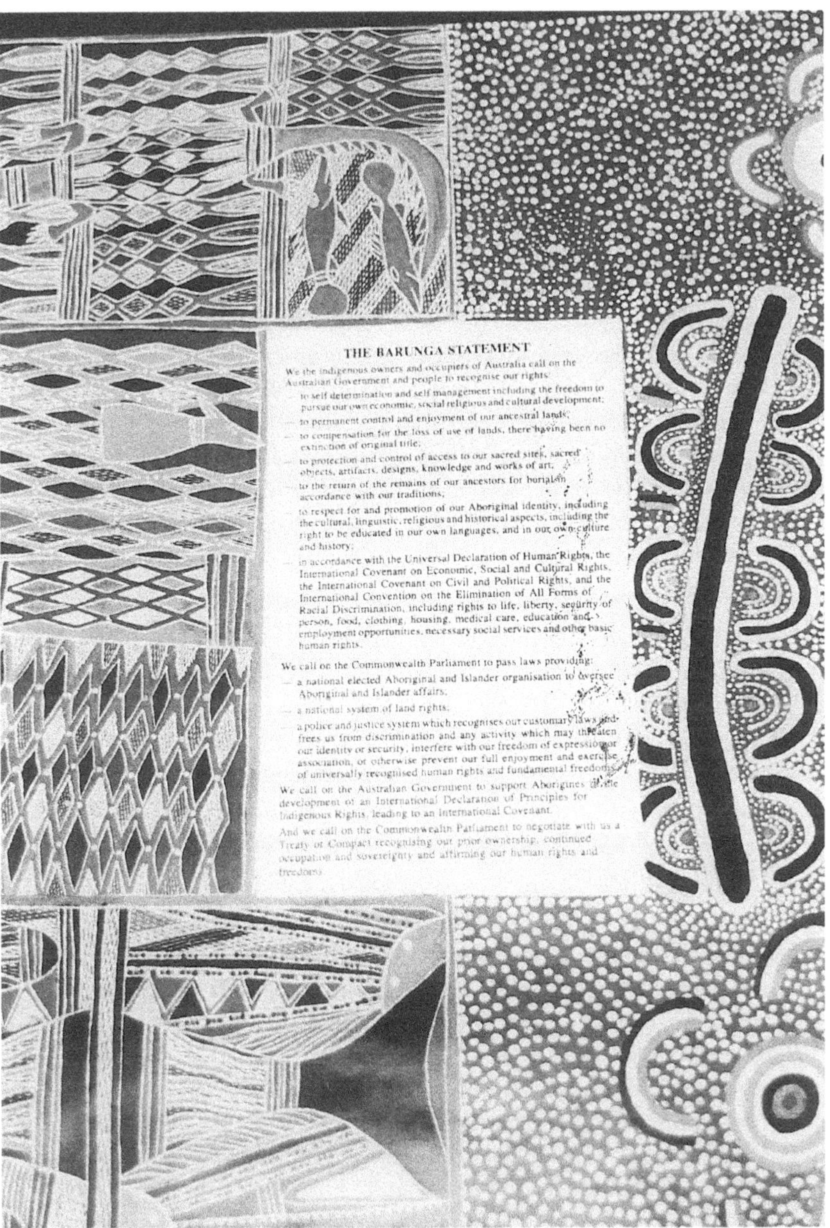

Figure 10.5
The Barunga Statement

The Wider World

The Barunga–Wugularr community has long integrated the wider world into its system of knowledge. This has been done not only through art and performances but also through film. Many of the artists from this region have claimed both national and international attention for the quality of their work. For example, David Blanarsi, Paddy Fordham Wainburranga and Peter Manabaru have been internationally recognised for their paintings on bark and other media and Joli Laiwongga has received acclaim for his compositions and performances as lead song-man. At the instigation of the entertainer Rolf Harris, a contingent of dances and musicians, including David Blanarsi, Joli Laiwongga and Jimmy Wesan, played at the opening of the Sydney Opera House in 1972. Harris' relationships with community members are recounted in popular books, such as *Rolf's Walkabout* (1972) and *Rolf Goes Bush* (1975). He had a particularly strong friendship with David Blanarsi, with whom he consorted in many countries, including England, Japan and the USA:

> My association with them began with David in 1967, when he was the first full-blood to make the trip to England since Bennelong went home with Phillip in 1792. David flew over for my television show [the *Rolf Harris Show*], stayed with us in London and loved it, said the house was a good place to camp, and mentioned that the television theatre would make a good cave. He was stunningly good on television, with tremendous dignity and humour and manhood coming through – a big hit.[26]

In addition to such outreach activities, many iconic films have been made in the general region of Barunga-Wugularr and have incorporated local talent. These films include Charles Chauvel's *Jedda, the Uncivilized* (1958), Cecil Holmes' *I, the Aboriginal* (1962) and Igor Auzins' *We of the Never Never* (1983). Apart from this, some actors have established national profiles. For example, Tommy Lewis, from Wugularr community, has film credits that include major roles in *A Town Like Alice* (1981) and *Robbery Under Arms* (1985) as well as the lead role in the Fred Schepsi film, *The Chant of Jimmie Blacksmith* (1980), which was based on the novel by Thomas Keneally. In *The Chant of Jimmie Blacksmith*, Tommy Lewis' character embodied the complexities of being an Aboriginal person of mixed descent who is searching for his cultural identity. Derived

Figure 10.6
Tommy Lewis and his mother Angelina George, the blue house, Wugularr, 2002

from real events, the film directly tackles issues of racism and cultural alienation, subjects that are as relevant today as they were when the film was released.

The wider world is incorporated into the lives of Barunga people in many ways. It is there in television shows and video. It is there in the ongoing presence of non-Indigenous people in their communities. It is there in the stories of returned travellers. But more than anything it is there in the Indigenous imperative to communicate, which arises from oral traditions that direct energies into sophisticated social structures, rather than into the development of material technologies. Since invasion, Indigenous people have taken advantage of whatever means are available to help them obtain and convey information. The material goods that Barunga people value most highly are telephones, televisions, videos, radios and cars – those technologies that enhance their ability to communicate with their lands, each other and the wider world. These are used by Aboriginal people to re-incorporate traditional lands into their lifestyles and to facilitate communal gatherings such as ceremonies and festivals.[27] This impetus to communicate places Aboriginal people in a powerful position to take advantage of the many possibilities provided by globalisation through radio, film, video, music and the Internet.

It is naïve to think of relationships between Barunga people and the wider world in terms of a unilineal imposition of European culture and values. The converse is closer to the truth, with senior Barunga people having a comprehensive agenda of educating the wider world about their belief systems and cultural values whenever the opportunity arises. This agenda is apparent is the following remarks made to researcher Kirsten Brett by Phyllis Wiynjorroc, Phillip Ashley and Peter Manabaru:

I'll be your teacher here and then [you] go home and tell stories and write a big book ... Tell the story in Adelaide school, Melbourne school and Canberra school.[28]

So whitefella can go back to their homes and tell all the people there what they have been learning.[29]

And mununga [whitefellas] read about put him in a book. You tell him read ... Not only blekbela kid, mununga kid got to know properly, too. So might be they can know next time. All the way along they got to know.[30]

Figure 10.7
Peter Manabaru teaching local school children about culture at Druphni excavation site near Barunga, 1999.
Photo G. Jackson

These remarks demonstrate that Barunga people have a clear role for researchers, who they see as cultural envoys whose job is to educate the wider world about the views of Aboriginal people. Relationships with the non-Aboriginal people who live in the same settlements are more complicated, as they are inhibited by the difficulties of communicating across cultures and the sparse knowledge most non-Aboriginal people have of Aboriginal systems of knowledge and power. These relationships are still structured by the different access to European power, knowledge and resources enjoyed by Aboriginal and non-Aboriginal people, even though Aboriginal

Figure 10.8
Phyllis Wiynjorroc teaching Flinders University students Sally May and Kirsten Brett about how stone tools were made in the old days, Barunga, 1998. Photo D. Flood

Figure 10.9
Research group from Flinders University taking their farewell, Barunga, 1998. Photo C. Smith

people have the right to revoke the permits of non-Aboriginal people who live on their lands. Most of the non-Aboriginal people living in Aboriginal settlements are in positions of authority; nurses, teachers or administrative staff and, beyond the needs of their jobs, there is not a lot of social interaction between them and the Aboriginal residents of the communities in which they live. This kind of social distance has been recorded since the 1960s. Maddock[31] comments that 'Long's observation on the Papunya settlement in Central Australia is equally applicable to Bamyili':

> In the settlement situation today the white community is large enough for its members to keep for the most part to themselves and they are inclined to maintain social distance between themselves and the native community.[32]

One problem with Long's statement is that he assumes that non-Aboriginal people maintain this social distance, failing to recognise that Aboriginal people also are inclined to minimise interactions between themselves and the non-Aboriginal community. While Barunga people regularly interact with local Europeans as part of their day-to-day existence, they rarely establish close friendships with them. Given the history of black–white relations in Australia, it is no surprise that Aboriginal people do not enthusiastically and indiscriminately embrace social relations with the transient white populations of their communities. On the contrary, most social interactions within the Barunga–Wugularr region are between Aboriginal people themselves. Though many Europeans live in the region as part of the administrative support structure, extended social interactions between Aboriginals and Europeans are rare. Those friendships between Aboriginals and Europeans that do develop generally involve Aboriginal people of mixed descent who can speak good English. Examples of friendships between the Aboriginal and non-Aboriginal inhabitants of these settlements are rare and such friendships rarely survive the European person's inevitable departure. For Barunga people, the relationships that will last a lifetime are those with the friends and family among whom they were born.

One of the regular conduits between Barunga people and the wider world is through Aboriginal visual and performing arts. Until recently, the arts of Indigenous Australians were little known and appreciated and for the most of the twentieth century were confined to the ethnographic sections of museums. The paintings were categorised as artefacts, traditional music and dance was recorded on tapes for academic audiences, and contemporary music and dance was virtually ignored. The production of paintings in natural pigments and on natural surfaces such as bark acted to have this work categorised 'primitive' and inhibited its adoption by a Western world that privileged material permanency. In fact, Aboriginal art only really entered the cultural mainstream once artists adopted permanent media such as paint and canvas, providing a permanent and portable art form which could be the subject of serious investment. Today, these art forms take their place in mainstream forums and are recognised internationally as extending the world's oldest continuous living cultural traditions.

The visual and performing arts of people in the Barunga–Wugularr region are part of the sophisticated ways of defining one's self, one's family and one's place in the world. These arts encompass drawings on bodies, rock and canvas as well as dance, music and song, each full of meaning. These cultural practices arise from complex social systems that communicate information about Aboriginal societies as a whole and about the place of particular individuals within those societies. Each art form is interdependent with the others and often a fusion of art forms may be necessary to express an idea properly. Aboriginal arts are inherently political, whether a bark painting or ceremonial rite that is actually a title deed to land, a dance that confronts the challenges of life in urban environments, a song that laments the loss of a stolen child, or a pandanus mat, the production of which is a testament to the importance of culture. The very existence of these arts is a statement of cultural survival.

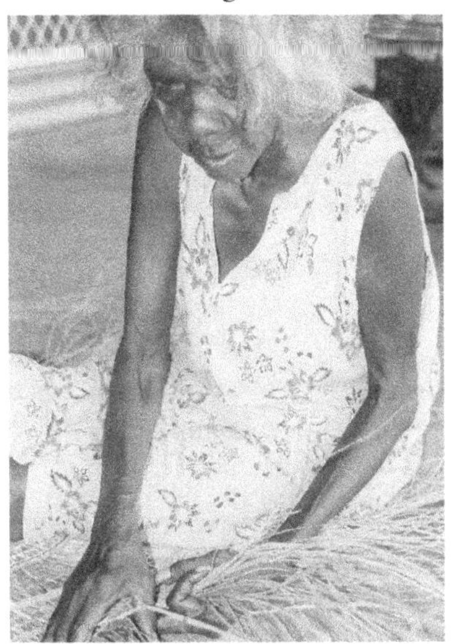

Figure 10.10
Glen Wesan working on a pandanus mat, Wugularr, 2003

One of the main ways in which Barunga people are shaping their futures is through their visual and performing arts. Whether they were produced in the past or the present, these arts are concerned with making connections between people and the world around them. They are an expression of ancestral relationships to land, an exploration of individual identity, protest against the injustices of colonialism – and, always, a statement of cultural survival.

The contemporary lives of Barunga people intersect with the wider world through metaphorical journeys via television and videos as well as through the lived experiences of people who have travelled to other places. Travelling has always been an important part of obtaining status in Indigenous societies, with the returned traveller bringing back new knowledge and extended social networks. This continues today, though in a modern form. People travel to many places in the world, for a range of reasons, such as being delegates to conferences or to accompany art exhibitions. Jimmy Wesan interprets the role of teaching culture in an international forum in terms of giving distinction not just for himself and his immediate family but for following generations, as well as providing an opportunity for senior people to focus on their culture and their forebears:

> We like to look at another country. We long enough in our own country, we might change that country, look around that country long way. [It's] good for old people because before I die I want to know that country. If I die, my son [is] going to say 'My father travelled all around the world', and all my daughters, like that. 'My father travelled around the world, talking culture, like that, because my father bin one of them culture people.' My son might [say that], or my daughter or my granddaughter.
>
> [It's] good because sometimes we never think about talk[ing] good way about culture. We think about it a little bit, but now we think about it a lot, what we do and what our father bin do before us.[33]

When the opportunity arises, Aboriginal people give travel a high priority in their lives. Their interest in other places, however, does not diminish the strength of their affection for their own lands. In November 2000, a group of five people from Barunga and Wugularr attended the annual meeting of the American Anthropological Association in San Francisco. Their reactions to the question 'What are you going to tell Barunga people about America?' show that

Figure 10.11
Participants in the 'Indigenous Voice' session at the 2000 meeting of the American Anthropological Association, San Francisco.
Jimmy Wesan, Peter Manabaru, Delma McCarthy, Darien Hood and Sybil Ranch in centre back row

travel, while interesting and worthwhile, also makes people feel satisfied with their own lives:

> Delma McCartney: Too big. Too many people, too many shop, too many motorcars. Too many aeroplanes, they have that traffic jam [in the sky]. Maybe five million people living in Los Angeles . . . We've been on them cable cars. We went to the beach and that sand was a different colour. It was a grey colour. The sand on the beach at Darwin is golden.
>
> Sybil Ranch: It's a busy place. Too many houses, too many freeways. It was a good thing, but we were confused about that money. How much is that dime worth? It was good to visit Disneyland. Pretty lights and we got photos to prove it!
>
> Darien Hood: We talked about our culture. We seen African and American dresses and all the baby clothes and those men [who] walked around the street with that tape [player] on their shoulder or in their arm. If we go back they won't believe us, but if you send that letter, they'll believe us.
>
> Jimmy Wesan: In my country I can know where I want to go. In America, I can't see where I'm going. I might get lost, like that. Too big.

> If I'm walking with my mate, or anybody, if I look around I might get lost, just like that (clicking his fingers). I can't see where he has gone because other people [have] come up. I can't see. I'll tell them it's a big country, that's all.[34]

Sybil Ranch, grand-daughter of Phyllis Wiynjorroc, also saw the trip in terms of cultural similarities and alliancing between Indigenous groups:

> We learnt about their culture and their beliefs. American Indian people. It was all right. That Marj has got that song that was handed down to her from her mother and grandmother and now she's got that story. That's the same way as Aboriginal people. Even though we [are] different race, creed and colour, we're still one. They got culture and we got culture.[35]

Barunga people are not only interested in visiting the wider world, but are also ready to have the wider world come to them for cultural training. Peter Manabaru and Jimmy Wesan[36] express their willingness to teach culture to both Aboriginal and non-Aboriginal people from throughout the world, as long as these people are amenable to be taught according to the strictures of Aboriginal law:

> PM: Might be we can tell young bloke, he should be learn about that you know young boy, cause old people, we are middle-aged people trying to teach the young people, you know, so he can get that culture from us. Yeah that's it, that's what we trying to do. No matter what him white or black, he still got to go you know, we just, we trying to learn him, not only, not only like white people from another different area, so that white people can find out about, from blackfella, from this territory.
>
> JW: We can [be] happy for that people, you know the old Aboriginal people, they might learn from us mob now, you know, we give them a talk you know, then we talk they might listen, they might listen 'Oh yes, it's good' like that . . . Yeah we can talk about this ceremony side, we can talk to ceremony side or might be once Aboriginal people come, come in the Northern Territory and we can learn 'em, and that ceremony side.
>
> PM: And they can believe in our culture.
>
> JW: They can believe in our culture.
>
> PM: They can see.
>
> JW: Not woman, not woman's side, but the men.

PM: Maybe from America, or from England, or from others like that you know . . . our story, they gotta just listen what we say alright now 'im say something about his culture now . . .

JW: They can listen what we say and might be, you know, well, we can say for young bloke or young girl like that, but you gotta have 'em [. . .?] you know old lady like they talking then culture side or anything, they might, they can learn 'em from this side [. . .?] country [?] like you do, that you learn 'em proper way, like Aboriginal way, we'll, they, gotta be same way. Because they're asking for that. They might believe us when we talk eh? The Aboriginal people we talk, from Malaysia, or from India, from, from, what do you call 'em? Not India but, I said that, what we call now? Africa, so they might listen what we, say, so might say 'Yeah, OK, that's good' you know, they might tell us 'Oh they're good'.

PM: They might ask him, they, people might ask him you know, you're Aboriginal this way if you want to try to learn [teach] some young bloke, we can easy, we'll do that and then they might do the same thing we do and then they all, we all together now and then teach other to all the young bloke, not only old fella, you know, old middle age, need properly young bloke you know. Oh not only young bloke, what about young girl? You can do that to them, you can control 'em then you know? They'll do it their own way it all you do, you gotta just do all the organising for them and they can [learn] and you can talk like all old middle-age people, young boy together. Young black, young white, learn from old middle-age people and old lady like, like my wife, like you do and young girl you know, young girl to learn about that culture.[37]

This conversation is illuminating in a number of ways. First, the willingness of these senior custodians of culture to teach the wider world is indicative of a view that would draw the wider world into their territory and convert its inhabitants to Indigenous rules. Second, the old men are laying the ground rules for the transmission of such knowledge. People have to learn the 'proper way', 'Aboriginal way'. This is evident in their discussion of how the knowledge would be taught, with men teaching men and women teaching women. This derives from and reinforces gender differentiation in knowledge (and, in practice, would have Europeans acting according to Aboriginal rules of behaviour). Thus, the possibility of teaching people from the wider world is in no way envisaged as impinging on traditional rules for transmitting knowledge. In these societies knowledge is owned and access to knowledge is something that has to be earned. There is no doubt that with the basic rules in place other cultural rules would also be implemented, keeping Indigenous cultural and intellectual property well within Indigenous ownership and control.

The importance of maintaining control over Indigenous cultural and intellectual property is a focus of contemporary political interest. While this is not protected adequately by existing legislation, this situation is due for change. In countries with Indigenous peoples there are a range of legislative changes being considered in order to accommodate Indigenous ways of knowing and of caring for knowledge. Such changes include revisions to recognise Indigenous knowledge in the development of new medicines; changing copyright legislation to recognise communal and multi-levelled ownership of designs and cultural knowledge; and re-writing legislation relating to performers rights so that it recognises the secret and restricted nature of certain Indigenous performances. All of these changes derive from traditional Aboriginal law. The protection of secret and restricted knowledge has always been an important issue for Aboriginal people.[38] In paintings, the secret is in the story rather than the image, as is apparent in the following comment by artist David Blanarsi about the publication of images:

> Might be you ask him, the juggayi girl or junggayi man 'Him got a meaning that story, this one?' and him say 'No, him no more gotta meaning story' because him shamed, 'cause if him give you that meaning him gonna get killed. 'Cause him working new way or something like that. Not these new people, long time before, might be some people still got that rule. I got that rule. I gada tell him straight 'no, you can't do that.' I gada think very quick and then I change him other way, make a different story. That picture you can see but that story him secret.
>
> If that story gada meaning we can't tell him, just leave him like that and don't talk that name, don't tell anyone. Just leave that picture in that book but no story, that's the way him go. Might be sometime you can put him. I got lot of story for that art, can't tell him name, sometime you might put him longa book and you put my name too, might be I get killed. Too many law.'[39]

Ironically, Europeans sometimes interpret the lack of accessible meaning in paintings as evidence that Aboriginal people have 'lost their culture'. The converse is true – the fact that the meanings are not given over to European consumption is not only evidence of the ongoing strength of Indigenous cultural practices but also continues to protect secret and restricted cultural knowledge.

Reconciliation

The formal beginning of the reconciliation process within Australia was marked by the *Aboriginal Reconciliation Act* of 1991. The Council had two main tasks. The first was to promote a deeper understanding by all Australians of the history, cultures, past dispossession and continuing disadvantage of Aboriginal and Torres Strait Islander peoples, and the need to redress that disadvantage. The second task was to consult Aboriginal and Torres Strait Islander people and the wider Australian community with a view to ascertaining how reconciliation might best be obtained.[40] Over the past decade it has provided an important voice in debates over Indigenous affairs. In discussion of the 1992 'Mabo' decision in the High Court of Australia, which recognised that Aboriginal and Torres Strait Islander peoples held a form of native title over the lands of Australia at the time of contact with Europeans, the Reconciliation Council pointed out that:

> it should be kept in mind that in many areas in the past actions of the Crown have dispossessed Aboriginal and Torres Strait Islander people without negotiation or compensation, leading to social, cultural and economic hardship that needs to be addressed.[41]

The infrastructure now exists for increased Aboriginal participation and control in most of these areas. ATSIC[42] points out that it was always apparent that dramatic improvements in employment and income levels would need to be accompanied, or even preceded, by equally dramatic transformations in the wider social and economic relations between Aboriginal and Torres Strait Islander and non-Indigenous peoples. It suggests that the developments of the past few years have not added up to a transformation as such but have contributed strongly to the circumstance in which such a transformation could occur. Certainly, the involvement of Aboriginal people in the decision making which directly concerns their own lives should assist in addressing some of the underlying causes relating to their disadvantaged socio-economic position within Australian society. These are matters over which Aboriginal people have the most intimate knowledge and concern.

Nevertheless, it is clear that the dynamism, flexibility and intelligence of Aboriginal people have not been enough to compensate for ongoing disadvantage in relation to land, housing, law and justice, cultural and intellectual property, education, employment, health, and economic development. Despite improvements in certain areas, enormous disparities still exist between the rights and living conditions of Indigenous and non-Indigenous Australians. Much needs to be done in order to redress entrenched historical inequities and to further the contemporary aspirations of Indigenous Australians. This need for reconciliation is discussed in a report submitted by ATSIC to the United Nations Human Rights Committee:

> The year 2000 is important in the relations between Indigenous and other Australians. The Reconciliation process, with its massive show of public support at the recent Corroborree 2000 activities in cities and towns around Australia, has highlighted the 'unfinished business' of Australian society, including an apology to Indigenous Australians for taking away Aboriginal children over many years (The Stolen Generations) and, more broadly, acknowledging the dispossession, destruction and disruption of Indigenous land, life and culture. The Reconciliation process entails not only restitution for past wrongs, but also the ongoing recognition and protection of Indigenous rights to land and culture.[43]

The contact history of the Barunga–Wugularr region is one of transformation, metamorphosis and ultimately survival. It is a history of strategic adaptation within an overall pattern of constraint, the realignment of social relations to ensure the continuity of core cultural concepts and the active incorporation of selected aspects of non-Aboriginal culture. Crucial and enduring concerns relate to the importance of country, kin and culture. The main facets of Western culture that were adopted by Barunga people are those economic items which make for easier day-to-day life – food, housing, and material goods that facilitate communication with country, kin and the wider world, such as cars, telephones and televisions. Aboriginal people became active agents who identified new opportunities and sought to make strategic changes in their lives. They decided that regular meals were preferable to the contingencies of bush living. They developed a new language, Kriol, in order to deal with the linguistic challenges of many language groups living in the one place. Once they had identified the value that Europeans placed on 'art', they took advantage of this opportunity for financial gain, but did so in a way that protected and restricted secret knowledge. The processes of community self-management and self-determination have been implemented in ways that are true to core values and which arise from, and reinforce, traditional social hierarchies and rights and responsibility to land. While there have been significant changes, the fundamental social structures and cultural laws, clearly grounded in Aboriginal systems of knowledge, have endured. In the words of Florrie Lindsay, the mother of Eileen Cummings:

> We still here yet.[44]

References

Aboriginal Deaths in Custody 1992 Overview of the Response by Governments to the Royal Commission. Canberra: Australian Government Publishing Service.

Austin, Tony 1989 Doomed to whither and disappear: Aboriginal and European relations in 1888. In V. Dixon (ed.) *Looking Back: The Northern Territory in 1888*. Darwin: Historical Society of the Northern Territory.

Austin, Tony 1990 Cecil Cook, Scientific Thought and 'Half Castes' in the Northern Territory 1927–1939. *Aboriginal History* 1–2:104–22.

Austin, Tony 1992 *Simply Survival of the Fittest. Aboriginal Administration in South Australia's Northern Territory 1863–1910*. Darwin: Historical Society of the Northern Territory.

Australian Bureau of Statistics 1991 *Census Counts. Selected Areas, Northern Territory. 1991 Census of Population and Housing*. Darwin: Australian Government Publishing Service.

Australian Bureau of Statistics 1994 *Housing Characteristics and Conditions*. Canberra: Commonwealth of Australia.

Australian Bureau of Statistics 1996 *Census of Population and Housing. Aboriginal and Torres Strait Islander People*. Canberra: Commonwealth of Australia.

Australian Government 1958 *Assimilation of Our Aborigines*. Canberra: Australian Government Printer.

Australian Government 1960 *The Skills of Our Aborigines*. Canberra: Australian Government Printer.

Australian Government 1961 *One People*. Canberra: Australian Government Printer.

Australian Government 1962a *Our Aborigines*. Canberra: Australian Government Printer.

Australian Government 1962b *Fringe Dwellers*. Canberra: Australian Government Printer.

Aboriginal and Torres Strait Islander Commission 1994 *Review of the Aboriginal Employment Development Policy*. Canberra: Aboriginal and Torres Strait Islander Commission.

Aboriginal and Torres Strait Islander Commission 2000 Aboriginal and Torres Strait Islander Peoples and Australia's Obligations under the United Nations International Covenant on Civil and Political Rights. A report submitted by the Aboriginal and Torres Strait Islander Commission to the United Nations Human Rights Committee.

Barta, Tony 1984 After the Holocaust: consciousness of genocide in Australia. *Australian Journal of Politics and History* 31(1):154–61.

Barta, Tony 1987 Relations of genocide. Land and lives in the colonisation of Australia. In M. Dobkowski and I. Wallimann (eds) *Genocide and the Modern Age*, pp. 237–51. New York: Greenwood.

Berndardi, Gus 1997 The Community Development Employment Projects (CDEP) Scheme: A case of welfare colonialism *Australian Aboriginal Studies* 2:36–46.

Berndt, Ronald and Catherine Berndt 1954 *Arnhem Land: its history and its people.* Melbourne: F.W. Cheshire.

Berndt, Ronald 1958 Some methodological considerations in the study of Australian Aboriginal art. *Oceania* 29:26–43.

Berndt, Ronald 1964 Preface. In R. Berndt (ed.) *Australian Aboriginal Art*, pp. 1–10. Sydney: Ure Smith.

Brady, Maggie 1992 *Heavy Metal. The Social Meaning of Petrol Sniffing in Australia.* Canberra: Aboriginal Studies Press.

Brady, Maggie 1998 *The Grog Book. Strengthening Indigenous Community Action on Alcohol.* Canberra: Commonwealth Department of Health and Family Services.

Brett, Kirsten 2001 Lenimbat Brom Jad Oldintaim En Tudei En Wek Bla Tumoro. A Community Education Approach: Towards a more relevant Indigenous archaeology. B.A. (Hons) thesis, Flinders University, South Australia.

Buck, Ronnie 1995 *Ronnie Buck. Bulman 1989.* Bulman Oral History Series. Barunga, Northern Territory: Barunga Press.

Butlin, N.G. 1983 *Our Original Aggression: Aboriginal populations of southeastern Australia 1788–1850.* Sydney: George Allen and Unwin.

Byler, W. 1977 The destruction of American Indian families. In Steven Unger (ed.) *The Destruction of American Indian Families.* New York: Association of American Indian Affairs.

Camfoo, Nelly 1995 *Nelly Camfoo. Bulman 1989.* Bulman Oral History Series. Barunga, Northern Territory: Barunga Press.

Camfoo, Tex 1995 *Tex Camfoo. Bulman 1989.* Bulman Oral History Series. Barunga, Northern Territory: Barunga Press.

Commonwealth of Australia 1937 Initial conference of Commonwealth and State Aboriginal Authorities. Canberra: Government Printer.

Cowlishaw, Gillian 1999 *Rednecks, Eggheads and Blackfellas. A Study of Racial Power and Intimacy in Australia.* Allen and Unwin, Sydney.

Cox, H.G. and C.M. n.d. *Our Floral Heritage, A Look at Northern Territory Wildflowers Embracing Two Cultures.* Palmerston, Australia.

Dalton, V. 1996 *Australian Deaths in Custody and Custody-related Police Operations 1995–96.* Canberra: Australian Institute of Criminology.

Dignan, Cecily and Roslyn Sharp 1996 *Sharing Good Tucker Stories.* Canberra: Commonwealth Department of Health and Family Services.

Farrell, David 1993 Preface. *A Time to Remember.* Armidale: unidentified printer.

Forrest, Peter 1985 An Outline of the History of Beswick Station and Related Areas. Unpublished manuscript held at the Northern Land Council, Darwin.

George, E. 1945 *Two at Daly Waters.* Melbourne: Georgian House.

George, Minnie 1995 *Minnie George. Bulman 1989.* Bulman Oral History Series. Barunga, Northern Territory: Barunga Press.

Gibbs, Alma 1995 *Alma Gibbs. Bulman 1989*. Bulman Oral History Series. Barunga, Northern Territory: Barunga Press.

Golvan, Colin 1996 Editorial: Turning point in copyright protection for Aboriginal art. *Media and Arts Law Review* 1:135–6.

Goodwin, C.D. 1964 Evolution theory in Australian social thought. *Journal of the History of Ideas* 25.

Greenhalgh, M. and V. Megaw (eds) 1978 *Art in Society: studies in style, culture and aesthetics*. London: Duckworth.

Hall, Rodney 1980 Aborigines, the Army and the Second World War in northern Australia. *Aboriginal History* 4(1):73–95.

Hall, Rodney 1992 Black Magic: Leonard Waters – Second World War fighter pilot. *Aboriginal History* 16:73–80.

Harlow, Sue 1992 A Social History of Mining at Maranboy. Unpublished B.A. (Hons) thesis, Northern Territory University.

Harlow, Sue 1997 *Tin Gods. A Social History of the Men and Women of Maranboy*. Darwin: Historical Society of the Northern Territory.

Harris, Rolf 1975 *Rolf Goes Bush*. Terrey Hills, Sydney: A.H. and A.W. Reed.

Hasluck, Paul 1997 *Mucking About: an autobiography*. Melbourne: Melbourne University Press.

Headon, D. 1991 *North of the Ten Commandments*. Sydney: Hodder and Stoughton.

Horton, David (ed.) 1994 *The Encyclopedia of Aboriginal Australia*. Canberra: Aboriginal Studies Press.

Human Rights and Equal Opportunities Commission 1997 *Bringing them Home. The National Inquiry into the Separation of Aboriginal and Torres Strait Islander Children from their Families*. Sydney: Human Rights and Equal Opportunities Commission.

Jangawanga, George 1995 In *Hitler Wood Katcherelli, George Jarudaku and George Jangawanga. Bulman 1991*, pp. 10–12. Bulman Oral History Series. Barunga, Northern Territory: Barunga Press.

Janke, Terri 1997 *Our Culture. Our Future. Proposals for the recognition of Indigenous cultural and intellectual property*. Discussion paper prepared for Australian Institute of Aboriginal Studies and the Aboriginal and Torres Strait Islander Commission.

Jaurdaku, George 1995 In *Hitler Wood Katcherelli, George Jarudaku and George Jangawanga. Bulman 1991*, pp. 4–9. Bulman Oral History Series. Barunga, Northern Territory: Barunga Press.

Jones, R. 1979 *Life on an Aboriginal Settlement. Bamyili, N.T.* Darwin: Northern Territory Department of Education.

Katcherelli, Hitler Wood 1995 In *Hitler Wood Katcherelli, George Jarudaku and George Jangawanga. Bulman 1991*, pp. 1–3. Bulman Oral History Series. Barunga, Northern Territory: Barunga Press.

Keen, Ian 1980 Alligator Rivers Stage II Land Claim. Unpublished manuscript held at the Northern Land Council, Darwin.

Langton, Marcia 1993 *Well, I Heard it on the Radio and I Saw it on the Television . . .* Sydney: Australian Film Commission.

Layton, Robert 2000 From clan symbol to ethnic emblem: indigenous creativity in a connected world. In C. Smith and G.K. Ward (eds) *Indigenous Cultures in an Interconnected World*, p. 49–66. Sydney: Allen and Unwin.

Lea, J.P. 1987 *Government and the Community in Katherine, 1937–1978*. Darwin: North Australia Research Unit, Australian National University.

Lee, Peter 1992 *Peter Lee. Bulman 1989*. Bulman Oral History Series. Barunga, Northern Territory: Barunga Press.

Letnic, Michael 2000 Along the Pituri Track. *Australian Geographic*. Apr–June issue.

Lindsay, Florrie 1995 *Florrie Lindsay and Dorothy Murray. Bulman 1989*. Bulman Oral History Series. Barunga, Northern Territory: Barunga Press.

Lovegrove, T.C. 1978 Legislation and Policies for Northern Territory Aboriginals over 27 years. Unpublished report submitted to the Northern Territory Department of Aboriginal Affairs.

Luthi, Bernhard and Gary Lee 1993 The Black/White Conflict. In *ARATJARA: Art of the First Australians*, Dusseldorf. Publication accompanying the exhibition ARATJARA: Art of the First Australians. Traditional and Conrtemporary Works by Aboriginal and Torres Strait Islander Artists.

Macintosh, N.G.W. 1952 Paintings at Beswick Creek Cave, Northern Territory. *Oceania* 22:256–74.

Maddock, Ken 1969 The Jabuduruwa. A study of the structure of rite and myth in an Australian Aboriginal religious cult on the Beswick Reserve, Northern Territory. Unpublished Ph.D. thesis, University of Sydney.

Maddock, Ken 1971 Imagery and social structure. *Anthropological Forum* 11:444–63.

Maddock, Ken 1982 *The Australian Aborigines*. Ringwood, Vic: Penguin Books.

Markus, Andrew 1990 *Governing Savages*. Sydney: Allen and Unwin.

McClay, David 1988 Surviving the White Man's World. Adult Education in Aboriginal Society. Unpublished Ph.D. thesis, University of Sydney.

McKeown, Frank 1992 The old paternalism: Queensland land rights from a Northern Territory perspective. *Australian Aboriginal Studies* 1:2–13.

Mercer, Colin 1997 'Creative Country'. Program Review of the ATSIC Arts And Crafts Industry Support Strategy (ACISS). Prepared For ATSIC, Canberra.

Merlan, Francesca 1978 Making people quiet in the pastoral north: reminiscences of Elsey Station. *Aboriginal History* 1(2):70–106.

Merlan, Francesca and Alan Rumsey 1982 The Jawoyn (Katherine Area) Land Claim. Unpublished manuscript held by the Northern Land Council, Darwin.

Michaels, Eric 1986 *The Aboriginal Invention of Television*. Canberra: Australian Institute of Aboriginal Studies.

Moizo, Bernard 1990 'Implememtation of the Community Development Employment Scheme in Fitzroy Crossing a Preliminary Report'. In B. Moizo *Australian Aboriginal Studies* 1:36–40.

Morphy, Howard 1983 'Now you understand': An analysis of the way Yolngu have used sacred knowledge to retain their autonomy. In N. Peterson and M. Langton (eds) *Aborigines, Land and Land Rights*, pp. 110–33. Canberra: Australian Institute of Aboriginal Studies.

Morphy, Howard 1991 *Ancestral Connections. Art and an Aboriginal System of Knowledge*. Chicago: The University of Chicago Press.

Mowbray, Malcolm 1986 State control or self-regulation?:on the political economy of local government in remote Aboriginal townships. *Australian Aboriginal Studies* 2: 31–39.

Mulvaney, Derek John 1989 *Encounters in Place*. St Lucia: University of Queensland Press.

Mulvaney, Derek John and Johann Kamminga 1999 *Prehistory of Australia*. Sydney: Allen and Unwin.

Northern Territory Department of Correctional Services 1992 Review of Aboriginal Community Justice Program. Unpublished manuscript held by the Northern Territory Department of Correctional Services, Darwin.

Northern Territory Law Reform Commission 1992 Alternative Dispute Resolution in Aboriginal Communities. A Discussion Paper. Unpublished manuscript held by the Northern Territory Law Reform Commission, Darwin.

Ogden, Pearl 1997 *Cowboy and his Acquaintances*. Winnellie, N.T.: Pearl Ogden.

O'Dea, K. 1991 *Traditional diet and food preferences of Australian Aboriginal hunter-gatherers*. Phil Trans of the Royal Society London 334:233–241.

O'Reilly, M.J. 1984 [1941] *Reminiscences of 40 years' Prospecting in Australia and Tasmania*. Carlisle, Western Australia: Hesperian Press.

Partington, Geoff 1996 *Hasluck vs Coombs*. Sydney: Quakers Hill Press.

Radcliffe-Brown, A.R. 1930 The Aboriginal population: former numbers and distribution of the Australian Aborigines. *Official Yearbook of the Commonwealth of Australia* 23:686–696.

Read, Peter 1981 *The Stolen Generations*. Sydney: New South Wales Government Printer.

Read, Peter 1999 *A Rape of the Soul so Profound*. Sydney: Allen and Unwin.

Read, Peter and Jay Read (eds) 1991 *Long Time, Olden Time: Aboriginal accounts of Northern Territory history*. Alice Springs: Institute for Aboriginal Development.

Reynolds, Henry 2000a *Black Pioneers. How Aboriginal and Islander people Helped Build Australia*. Ringwood: Penguin.

Reynolds, Henry 2000b *Why Weren't we Told? A Personal Search for the Truth about our History*. Ringwood: Penguin.

Reynolds, Henry 2001 *An Indelible Stain? The Question of Genocide in Australia's History*. Ringwood: Viking.

Robinson, Bandicoot 1995 *Bandicoot Robinson. Bulman 1989*. Bulman Oral History Series. Barunga, Northern Territory: Barunga Press.

Rose, Deborah Bird 1991 *Hidden Histories*. Canberra: Aboriginal Studies Press.

Rose, Deborah Bird 1992 *Dingo Makes Us Human: life and land in an Australian Aboriginal culture*. Cambridge: Cambridge University Press.

Rose, Deborah Bird 1996 *Nourishing Terrains. Australian Aboriginal Views of Landscapes and Wilderness*. Canberra: Australian Heritage Commission.

Royal Commission into Aboriginal Deaths in Custody 1991 National Report. Volume 5. Recommendations. Canberra: Australian Government Publishing Service.

Rowley, C.D. 1986 *The Politics of Aboriginal Reform*. Ringwood: Penguin Books.

Rowse, Tim 1993 *After Mabo: interpreting indigenous traditions*. Melbourne: Melbourne University Press.

Rowse, Tim 2000 *Obliged to be Difficult. Nugget Coombs' Legacy in Indigenous Affairs*, 2000. Cambridge University Press.

Sandefur, J.R. and J.L. Sandefur 1982 *An Introduction to Conversational Kriol*. Darwin: Summer Institute of Linguistics, Australian Aborigines Branch.

Serventy, Carol and Alwen Harris 1972 *Rolf's Walkabout*. 2nd reprinting. Adelaide: A.H. and A.W. Reed for Rigby Ltd.

Smith, Claire 1992 Executive producer, *Jungayi. Caring for Country*. Documentary video. Copyright held by Jawoyn Association.

Smith, Claire and Graeme K. Ward (eds) 2000 *Indigenous Cultures in an Interconnected World*. Sydney: Allen and Unwin.

Smith, Claire and Gary Jackson 2000 Wugularr Community Management Plan 2000–2005. Unpublished report to Wugularr Community Government Council.

Tickner, Robert 1992 *Social Justice for Indigenous Australians*. Canberra: Australian Government Publishing Service.

Tindale, Norman 1974 *Aboriginal Tribes of Australia*. Canberra: Australian National University Press.

Welfare Branch, Northern Territory 1961 Beswick Aboriginal Reserve. Unpublished manuscript held at the Northern Land Council, Darwin.

Welfare Branch, Northern Territory 1967 Beswick Aboriginal Reserve. Unpublished manuscript held at the Northern Land Council, Darwin.

Williams, Nancy 1979 Australian Aboriginal art at Yirrkala: the introduction and development of marketing. In N. Graburn (ed.) *Ethnic and Tourist Arts: cultural expressions from the fourth world*, pp. 266–84. Berkeley: University of California Press.

Newspapers and Newsletters

Barunga: Bamyili Community Newsletter

Northern Territory Times and Gazette

Sydney Morning Herald

The Australian

The Melbourne Age

Unpublished Archival Sources

Australian Archives (Darwin)

Annual Report by the Government Resident on the Administration of the Territory of Central Australia for the year 1st July, 1929, to 30th June, 1930.

Annual Report by the Government Resident on the Administration of the Territory of Central Australia for the year 1st July, 1938, to 30th June, 1939.

CRS F1 52/775 (I)	Beswick Creek
CRS F1 52/839	Beswick Creek – general
CRS F1 55/363	Native school and residence Beswick Creek
CRS F1 1942/415	Employment of Aborigines in Army labour gangs
CRS F1 1946/820 (I)	Beswick
CRS F1 1949/279	Beswick Station
CRS F1 1943/85	Labour on the Maranboy tinfield
CRS F1 1949/113	Proposed Native Settlement Maranboy Area Tandangal
CRS F315 49/393A (I)	Patrol Reports
CRS F315 49/393A (III)	Maranboy

Northern Territory Archives (Darwin)

F297	Katherine Police Journal 1939

Notes

Chapter 1

1 See Mulvaney and Kamminga 1999

2 It is very difficult for archaeologists or anthropologists to determine the nuances of how social systems worked in the past. This part of this chapter is based upon the social structures and relationships that exist in Barunga societies today, extrapolated into the past on the assumption that such complex relationships must have taken many millenia to evolve.

3 The word Dreamtime is not used as much today as it was in the past, and people feel that it tends to trivalise Indigenous belief systems. Also, from a European worldview it seems to represent a lack of reality, whereas for Indigenous people it represents an ultimate reality.

4 1974

5 1994

6 cited in Merlan 1978:76

7 Radcliffe Brown 1930

8 Butlin 1983

9 e.g. Mulvaney 1989:xv; Rose 1992:7

10 Tickner 1992:12

11 Butlin 1983

12 Rose 1992:7

13 Keen 1980:171

14 Mulvaney 1989:128

15 Rose 1992:9

16 1984, 1987

17 2001

18 Barta 1987:239

19 cited in Austin 1992:23

20 Mulvaney 1989:128

21 cited in Austin 1989:86
22 Goodwin 1964:398
23 cited in Austin 1992:31
24 Jaurdaku 1995:4–5
25 Interview with CS November 2001
26 Jaurdaku 1995:6
27 Jaurdaka 1995:7–8
28 Interview with CS, June 1993
29 Robinson 1995:1–4
30 see Mulvaney 1989:128, in regards to the masking of comparable incidents in central Australia
31 F297 Katherine Police Journal 1939

Chapter 2

1 Hasluck 1997:210
2 *Sydney Morning Herald*, December 1921
3 see Lovegrove 1978:5
4 F315 49/393A Part 1
5 F1 1949/113
6 Annual Report by the Government Resident on the Administration of the Territory of Central Australia for the Year 1st July, 1929, to 30th June, 1930
7 Harlow 1997:10
8 Harlow 1997:13
9 O'Reilly 1984[1941]:71; Harlow 1997:37
10 Forrest 1985:4
11 Report on the Administration of the Northern Territory for Year 1938–39
12 Harlow 1992:45
13 Interview with CS February 1999
14 Merlan and Rumsey 1982:22
15 see Reynolds 2000a
16 1992:6–7
17 1984[1941]:72
18 Interview with CS June 1993
19 Harlow 1992:44
20 F1 A194, cited in Merlan and Rumsey 1982: 24
21 cited in Read and Read 1991:110
22 George 1945:26
23 O'Reilly 1984[1941]:73
24 Interview with CS January 1992
25 see, for example, various stories in Headon 1991; Read and Read 1991; Austin 1992; Rose 1991, 1992
26 see O'Reilly 1984[1941]:72
27 Daisy Borduk interview with CS, June 1993
28 Interview with CS May, 1999
29 1984[1941]:72
30 F1 1943/85
31 F1 1943/85

32 Interview with CS November 2001
33 In Headon 1991:146
34 F1 1942/415
35 F1 1942/415
36 1992:78
37 Camfoo 1995:3
38 cf. Hall 1980

Chapter 3

1 1954:21
2 see discussion in Lea 1987
3 1987:81
4 F315 49/393A Part 1
5 Merlan and Rumsey 1982:25
6 F1 1949/113
7 F1 49/393A Part 1
8 Interview with CS, September 1999
9 F1 1949/113
10 Merlan and Rumsey 1982:28
11 F1 1949/113
12 F1 52/775 Part 1
13 Interview with CS June 2000
14 Interview with CS June 2000
15 F315 49/393A Part 1
16 F1 49/393A Part 1
17 F1 52/775 Part 1
18 F1 49/393A Part 1
19 F1 52/474 Part 1

Chapter 4

1 1995:3–4
2 CS interview with David Blanarsi, March 2000
3 Forrest 1985:4
4 CS interview with Daisy Borduk, September 1993
5 Ogden 1997:19
6 1985:5
7 see also Merlan and Rumsey 1982:30
8 CS interview with Daisy Borduk September 1993
9 CS interview with Peter Manabaru May 1999
10 Ogden 1997:19
11 Ogden 1997:19
12 Interview with CS March 2000
13 F1 1946/820 Part 1
14 F1 55/363
15 F1 1949/279
16 Gibbs 1995:1
17 F315 49/393A part1

18 F1 52/543
19 F1 1946/820 Part 1
20 F1 1946/820 Part 1
21 F1 1946/820 Part 1
22 F1 1946/820 Part 1
23 Annual Report 1953 Beswick Station
24 F1 52/768
25 Gibbs 1995:11
26 Interview with CS May 1993

Chapter 5

1 F1 52/775 Part 1
2 ca.1978:8
3 Cowlishaw 1999:179
4 F1 54/1013
5 Australian Government 1958
6 Australian Government 1960
7 Australian Government 1961
8 Australian Government 1962a
9 Australian Government 1962b
10 Australian Government, 1962a:8
11 Interview with CS June 1999
12 Australian Government 1961
13 F1 52/775 Part 1
14 Welfare Branch, N.T. 1967
15 Interview with CS June 1999
16 1995:6–7
17 Interview with CS May 1999
18 Welfare Branch, N.T. 1967:16
19 Jones 1979:7
20 1967:15

Chapter 6

1 Welfare Branch, N.T. 1961
2 Australian Government 1962b:11
3 F1 52/839
4 F1 49/393
5 F1 52/839
6 Minnie George 1995:5
7 1995:6–7
8 Maddock 1971:457
9 1969:43, 45
10 Welfare Branch, N.T. Administration 1961
11 Welfare Branch, N.T. Administration 1967
12 1969:46–7
13 CRS F1 54/87
14 Interview with CS April 1999

15 Minnie George 1995:2–3
16 1999:173
17 F1 63/3200 June 1960, quoted in Cowlishaw 1999:173
18 CS interview with Rocky Cameron June 2000
19 Welfare Branch, N.T. 1961

Chapter 7

1 Read 1981
2 UN Document E/447 (1947), quoted in Human Rights and Equal Opportunities Commission 1997:271
3 UN Document A/AC6/SR83 (1948) at 195, quoted in Human Rights and Equal Opportunities Commission 1997:271
4 Human Rights and Equal Opportunities Commission 1997:5
5 Byler 1977
6 1999:161
7 Read 1999:67
8 Austin 1990
9 Commonwealth of Australia 1937:10
10 Commonwealth of Australia 1937:14
11 Markus 1990:98
12 Interview with CS June 2000
13 1999:169
14 Reynolds 2000b
15 Commonwealth of Australia 1937
16 Hitler Wood Katcherelli 1995:1
17 T. Camfoo 1995:1
18 Jangawanga 1995:10–11
19 Human Rights and Equal Opportunities Commission 1997:253
20 Interview with CS May 1999
21 Interview with CS April 1999
22 Ibid
23 F315, Item 49/393A, Part 1
24 Interview with CS April 1999
25 Interview with CS May 1999
26 Ibid
27 Interview with CS April 1999
28 Human Rights and Equal Opportunities Commission 1997:260
29 Lorraine Siwers interview with CS May 1999
30 Interview with CS January 2001
31 Interview with CS May 1999
32 Human Rights and Equal Opportunities Commission 1997:259
33 Human Rights and Equal Opportunities Commission 1997:262
34 Interview with CS May 1999
35 Ibid
36 Commonwealth of Australia 1937:17
37 Interview with CS May 1999
38 Commonwealth of Australia 1937:14

39 Interview with CS May 1999
40 Ibid
41 Human Rights and Equal Opportunities Commission 1997:177
42 Human Rights and Equal Opportunities Commission 1997:260
43 Interview with CS May 1999
44 Interview with CS January 2001
45 Interview with CS May 1999
46 Interview with CS January 2001
47 Human Rights and Equal Opportunities Commission 1997:212
48 Interview with CS February 1999
49 Interview with CS, at Werrenbun, 27th February, 2003
50 Human Rights and Equal Opportunities Commission 1997:304
51 Human Rights and Equal Opportunities Commission 1997:200
52 Interview February 1999
53 Interview with CS, 26th February, 2003.
54 Read 1999:106–7
55 Interview with CS January 2001

Chapter 8

1 Northern Territory Office of Local Government 1988:2
2 see Bennett 1985
3 Interview with CS February 1999
4 Lovegrove ca. 1978:11–12
5 McKeown 1992
6 CS interview with Jimmy Wesan, February 1999
7 see *Barunga: Bamyili Community Newsletter No.2* 1984
8 Berndardi 1997:36
9 See, for example, Moizo 1999
10 Ibid, p.40
11 Mowbray 1986:38
12 Cowlishaw 1999:265
13 Rowse 2000:84
14 cf. Rowse 2000:140
15 In T. Rowse 2000:139

Chapter 9

1 1975:455, quoted in McClay 1988:2
2 In census estimates the total population includes Indigenous people, non-Indigenous people and people who do not identify as either.
3 Australian Bureau of Statistics 1996:5; ATSIC 1994:17
4 Australian Bureau of Statistics 1996:2
5 Australian Bureau of Statistics 1996:4
6 Australian Bureau of Statistics 1996:47
7 Smith and Jackson 2000:53.
8 ATSIC 1994:17
9 Interview with CS September 1999
10 ATSIC 1994:18

11 Tickner 1992:9
12 Australian Bureau of Statistics 1991:68
13 Northern Territory Department of Health and Community Services 1992:18
14 Dignan and Sharp 1996:19
15 ATSIC 1994:18
16 Dignan and Sharp 1996:17
17 Dignan and Sharp 1996:17
18 Dignan and Sharp 1996:20
19 Australian Bureau of Statistics 1991:39
20 Australian Bureau of Statistics 1991:40–41
21 Northern Territory Department of Health and Community Services 1992:iii
22 Australian Bureau of Statistics 1994:1
23 Australian Bureau of Statistics 1991:52
24 Northern Territory Department of Health and Community Services 1992:19
25 Australian Bureau of Statistics 1994:46
26 Australian Bureau of Statistics 1994:30
27 Australian Bureau of Statistics 1991:61
28 Australian Bureau of Statistics 1996:20
29 Smith and Jackson 2000
30 Interview with CS November 1992
31 Interview with CS September 1999
32 Brady 1998:211–15
33 Brady 1998:1
34 Brady 1998:1
35 Letnic 2000:109
36 Brady 1998:12
37 Ibid, p.41
38 Ibid, p.12
39 Ibid, p.14
40 Aboriginal Deaths in Custody. 1992:1
41 1995:10
42 see Brady 1992
43 In Brett 2000:43
44 Smith and Jackson 2000
45 1969:43, 45
46 Interview with CS September 1999
47 see, for example, discussion Northern Territory Law Reform Committee 1992
48 Dalton 1996 Table 3
49 Northern Territory Law Reform Committee 1992:9
50 Australian Bureau of Statistics 1996:p.2
51 Royal Commission into Aboriginal Deaths in Custody 1991 Recommendations 328–333
52 Ibid, Volume 1, para 1.7.6
53 Ibid, recommendation 2.8
54 Northern Territory Department of Correctional Services 1992:6
55 Northern Territory Law Reform Committee 1992:14
56 Ibid 1992:7

57 CS interview with Phyllis Wijnjorroc September 1992
58 Royal Commission into Aboriginal Deaths in Custody 1991:358
59 Interview with CS May 1999
60 Jimmy Wesan, quoted in Brett 2000:47
61 Community dissatisfaction with mandatory sentencing has been mooted as one factor in the recent electoral loss by the Country Liberal Party alliance, see the Australian, 22nd August, 2001.
62 Aboriginal and Torres Strait Islander Commission 2000:24
63 Ibid, p. 20
64 Ibid, p. 24

Chapter 10

1 Luthi and Lee 1993:66
2 Interview with CS February 2000
3 see Layton 2000
4 see Sandefur and Sandefur 1982
5 In Brett 2001, appendices, interview minidisk 5, track 7
6 In Brett 2001, appendices, interview minidisk 8, track 18
7 Interview with CS May 1991
8 Cited in Rose 1996: 14
9 Smith 1992
10 see also Macintosh 1952
11 see also Maddock 1969:43, 45
12 Interview with CS June 1993
13 Interview with CS August 1991
14 1982:36
15 1971
16 Maddock 1982:94
17 Ibid, p.94
18 1978b:xiii
19 1958:27
20 see also Williams 1979:270
21 Berndt 1964:1
22 for an excellent discussion of the role in Aboriginal social and political life see Morphy 1991
23 Mercer 1997
24 2001:49
25 see Morphy 1983 for a detailed discussion ofYolngu using paintings for political purposes.
26 Harris 1975:7
27 Langton 1993:63; Michaels 1986:5
28 Phyllis Wiynjorroc in Brett 2001:96
29 Phillip Ashley in Brett 2001:96
30 Peter Manabaru in Brett 2001:96
31 1969:42–3
32 Cited in Maddock 1969:43
33 Interview with CS November 2000 at Disneyland, Los Angeles

34 Interview with CS November 2000 at Disneyland, Los Angeles
35 Interview with CS November 2000 at Disneyland, Los Angeles
36 Interview with CS October 1998
37 Interview with CS October 1998
38 Golvan 1996; also see discussion in Janke 1997
39 Interview with CS February 2000
40 Tickner 1992:22
41 Commonwealth of Australia 1993:94
42 1994:37
43 Aboriginal and Torres Strait Islander Commission 2000:4
44 Lindsay 1995:5

Index

Wakefield Press is an independent publishing and distribution company based in Adelaide, South Australia. We love good stories and publish beautiful books. To see our full range of books, please visit our website at www.wakefieldpress.com.au where all titles are available for purchase. To keep up with our latest releases, news and events, subscribe to our monthly newsletter.

Find us!

Facebook: www.facebook.com/wakefield.press
Twitter: www.twitter.com/wakefieldpress
Instagram: www.instagram.com/wakefieldpress

www.ingramcontent.com/pod-product-compliance
Ingram Content Group Australia Pty Ltd
76 Discovery Rd, Dandenong South VIC 3175, AU
AUHW010840020625
411871AU00001B/1

9 781862 545755